PAST LIVES – PRESENT HEALING

A Fascinating Collection Of Past Life Experiences

DEBORAH J. MONSHIN

"What we do in life echoes through eternity"

'Gladiator' (Ridley Scott, Universal Studios 2001)

TRAFFORD

• Canada • UK • Ireland • USA •

Note for Librarians: A cataloguing record for this book is available from Library and Archives Canada at www.collectionscanada.ca/amicus/index-e.html
ISBN 1-4120-8385-0

Printed in Victoria, BC, Canada. Printed on paper with minimum 30% recycled fibre. Trafford's print shop runs on "green energy" from solar, wind and other environmentally-friendly power sources.

TRAFFORD
PUBLISHING™
Offices in Canada, USA, Ireland and UK
This book was published *on-demand* in cooperation with Trafford Publishing. On-demand publishing is a unique process and service of making a book available for retail sale to the public taking advantage of on-demand manufacturing and Internet marketing. On-demand publishing includes promotions, retail sales, manufacturing, order fulfilment, accounting and collecting royalties on behalf of the author.

Book sales for North America and international:
Trafford Publishing, 6E–2333 Government St.,
Victoria, BC v8t 4p4 CANADA
phone 250 383 6864 (toll-free 1 888 232 4444)
fax 250 383 6804; email to orders@trafford.com
Book sales in Europe:
Trafford Publishing (uk) Limited, 9 Park End Street, 2nd Floor
Oxford, UK oxi 1hh UNITED KINGDOM
phone 44 (0)1865 722 113 (local rate 0845 230 9601)
facsimile 44 (0)1865 722 868; info.uk@trafford.com
Order online at:
trafford.com/06-0140

10 9 8 7 6 5 4 3

CONTENTS

For my daughters, Natalie & Christina, who support me, come what may, and, to all those souls who are determined to discover who they really are. May this book guide and support you on your own spiritual quest.

WHAT THEY SAY:

"Anyone interested in the self-discovery that occurs from exploring past lives should most definitely read 'Past Lives – Present Healing.' With a voice of wisdom, born of extensive experience and training, Deborah gently, yet profoundly, nudges you to step into your past with safety and certainty. This remarkable journey into the past can truly heal your present life. I recommend this book!"—**Denise Linn**, author of 'Past Lives – Present Dreams'.

"As a practising hypnotherapist for over 15 years, I have read many books on past lives, and must say this is one of very few that I have not wanted to put down. Very, very, good!"—**Dominic Beirne**, C.M.H. C.hyp MPNLP Dominic Beirne School of Clinical Hypnosis and Psychotherapy.

"In the forty years I have been involved in past lives, I still found something new in this book. I recommend this book for experienced therapists and novices alike. This work is an important new contribution to the field of regression therapy filled with fascinating case histories using real clients. If authors like Deborah can share their insights into some of the exciting features that comprise the evolutionary step in our ability to access and interact with past life data as well as how easy and rewarding it is, then perhaps more people will discover a hidden passion for discovering their genesis." **Vicki Watson**, Founder of the National Society of Professional Hypnotherapists.

FOREWORD

Having been involved with hypnotherapy and past life regression for over four decades and facilitated training courses for over ten years it is inevitable that you develop an intuitive understanding of your clients and students at a very early stage in your relationship with them.

I first met Deborah Monshin some years ago when she attended our Clinical Hypnotherapy Training Course, which also incorporated exploring past life regression via several techniques, that I administered. The freshness of her outlook was immediately apparent, as was her insatiable desire to learn, her need to understand and analyse information put before her, plus her dedication to providing a 'duty of care' to everyone she worked with during the course.

Now a skilled practitioner, Deborah demonstrates a deep understanding and remarkable resolve, through the medium of her book, to help other practitioners comprehend how to take benefit from the many past-life techniques available to them for their own use and for use with prospective clients.

Her empathy for and profound consideration of the needs of practitioners are clearly apparent as she takes the time to explain the case study scenarios that design decisions and follows it up with an interpretation on how healing takes place in the life the individual is living at this present time, which I believe will help both experienced therapists and novices. Having read her book from beginning to end, I recommend that you do the same because the case studies provide valuable context.

The benefits of the author's personal experiences, as well as those of the contributors to the book, show through in this book's unique client perspective of the evolution of their spirit through their past lives as described in 'Past Lives – Present Healing.'

If authors like Deborah Monshin can share their insights into some of the exciting features that comprise the evolutionary step in our ability to access and interact with past life data as well as how easy and rewarding it is, then perhaps more people will discover a hidden passion for discovering their genesis.

This work is an important new contribution to the field of regression therapy filled with fascinating case histories involving the experiences of real people. Exploration of the lives we have lived prior to this one we are in at present extensively augments the riveting journey of the soul in its search for healing of chronic problems, self-discovery and elucidation. As the author reiterates time and again, awareness and comprehension of former incarnations can turn into a enthralling journey of self-discovery and healing of many long term chronic illnesses, aches and pains, ingrained bad habits, destructive fears and phobias as well as problems such as persistent obesity.

One important area that is explored is Spiritual Regression. This is where the therapist, after guiding the client through a past life, then leads them into the spirit world "between" lives. The importance of this is to alleviate the fear of death that countless people have and while the past-life experience is truly amazing in itself, the goal of a spiritual regression is to allow the subject to see, feel and know what happens to us after we die and return to the spirit world.

Ultimately, there really is no substitute for learning by doing, in relation to healing old hurts, traumas, chronic illnesses, unsocial habits, etc., through the treatment modality of Past Life Regression. Deborah demonstrates that in the case studies she has chosen for inclusion in this book. I believe that all readers of this book as well as Past Life Regression practitioners will benefit from Deborah's experience and her ability to communicate that well.

Vicki Watson RGN FNCP SQHP MGHR Founder of the National Society of Professional Hypnotherapists www.nsph-hypnotherapy.co.uk

INTRODUCTION

Whether you believe in reincarnation or not is not important, remaining open to the possibility is.

This is a book about regular people who have recalled memories of their past lives. Each one has overcome or healed long-term emotional and in some cases, physical problems by accessing these past life memories and resolving the difficult decisions or attitudes they held at the time. The past life has been recalled and re-experienced allowing the traumas to be processed. Understanding is achieved by placing these experiences in context and learning the lessons required, in order to move forward.

All the people who have shared their stories with me, and now you, have overcome difficulties and have experienced healing as a direct result of accessing these past life memories. This is something remarkable: it cannot be ignored or dismissed as fantasy. These people have experienced something wonderful in their lives: they have each progressed on their personal journey and they have learnt more about themselves. The past life memories inside this book are all very different, but one thing that all the contributors discovered, is that they are no longer afraid to die.

Within, is a collection of their past life recollections and the healing that occurred.

I hope that everyone who reads this book learns something from each contributor's story. I hope that each of you is inspired by their personal experiences and that you are encouraged to open your hearts and minds to embrace your own spiritual journey.

I have written this book for people who are curious about past lives and who want to know more about the process and the benefits;

For those who are familiar with past lives but would like more information on a personal level before deciding perhaps, to experience a past life for themselves;

For those people who prefer alternative therapies and who may be looking for resolution for long-term problems, maybe for which they have tried the conventional healing route, without success and

For therapists, novices and experienced alike, who may find the detailed approach to problem solving useful for their own practices.

Although I personally believe in past lives and reincarnation, I feel this is not essential when exploring the possibility of a past life. What matters is that the insights you gain during the process and the knowledge you learn about yourself helps to heal any trauma and takes you further along the path of spiritual enlightenment. Once regressed, any scepticism usually vanishes, as the experience is unlike any other you may encounter.

This book is a collection of personal experiences that illustrates what can, and what has happened when we remain open to the possibilities.

These are important stories that are waiting to be heard.

CHAPTER ONE

PAST LIVES – HEALING THE SOUL

"Death is like a door left ajar –
it allows us the choice of returning"

Deborah

PAST LIVES – HEALING THE SOUL

PAST LIFE REGRESSION

Have we lived before? How can we find out?

It is not necessary to believe but to remain open in order to learn.

Exploration or therapy? Past Life regression is a means of discovering more about our inner selves. What motivates us? What holds us back? What makes us afraid? Why are we instantly attracted to some people and repelled by others? Why do we get on with some family members whilst other relationships are fraught with difficulties?

Traditional psychology sees each person as being born as a 'Tabula Rasa': a blank sheet, where genetics, experience and environment produce the personality that we have as adults. However, the possibility of reincarnation allows a much wider view. Reincarnation takes into consideration previous life experiences and their accumulative effect upon the present incarnation.

As every observant parent knows, a child's character and personal preferences are already developed by the time of birth. For example, why does one baby sleep peacefully and regularly, waking only for food; and another cry persistently and demand a lot of attention? Why is one toddler content to amuse himself at play, and another is fractious in nature and constantly wants company? Even in the womb babies behavioural patterns differ, from those that move more during the day than in the night; those that kick rather than roll; those that have definite food preferences and those that respond to different kinds of music and other external stimuli.

Likewise, why does a toddler have an intense fear of water with no apparent cause in this lifetime?

Why does a four-year-old scream in terror every time he is put into a car seat? How can a six-year-old talk, with authority, about places he visited and experiences he had "When I was big"?

Allowing for the probability of reincarnation gives us greater understanding of the purpose of the soul and our current understanding and experiences of this lifetime. Reincarnation also helps us to accept that we are part of the world around us, not isolated components within it.

A past life regression can be used for purely exploratory purposes or as a gateway to discover the reasons behind long-term problems. For example, causes of some food addictions and binge eating have successfully been traced to previous lifetimes of poverty and starvation. Some relationship difficulties may be traced back to a previous lifetime where betrayal or abuse was a major issue, or where intense love and loyalty created problems in the current lifetime, such as promises made to lovers and family that couldn't be kept. Many phobias and fears may also relate back to tragic events or accidents in a past life.

Whether for light-hearted exploration or for seeking answers to more serious issues, delving into past lives can bring many rewards from recalling previous skills and talents, being present at key events in history, resolving minor health complaints, or experiencing a deeply content and happy lifetime.

All these discoveries can have a profound and healing effect on our current life. An emotion that arose as a result of a trauma in a past life and was subsequently suppressed, can create a problem or phobia in the current life. Likewise, a decision may have been made in a past lifetime that has been carried forward for example: "I'll never trust a man again!" or "That's the last time I'll go near a horse", or "I'll never waste food again."

As a holistic therapist I have had many years experience of guiding clients through their past lives, helping them to resolve conflict and trauma. Once these traumas have been recalled, explored and resolved, that past life can give the client invaluable information about the lessons they needed to learn, and usually provides insights into problems or questions they have regarding their current life choices.

If you are looking to resolve issues, it's important to first explore the current life for traumas that may have caused the problem, or that may have contributed to it. Initially going to a past life for the answer may not be appropriate if the past life wasn't the cause. It is not necessarily a physical trauma or event that has affected current behaviour, but often the emotion or belief attached to that trauma.

Frequently what surfaces in a past life regression isn't what the client expected as the unconscious mind chooses and accesses what is relevant at any given time. A different memory may need to be relieved before the appropriate past life can be accessed. But all information is valuable and relevant, and will be remembered. Everything learned and observed is integrated into the conscious mind to help improve the quality of our lives and the understanding we have of ourselves and the people around us.

HEALING THE PRESENT

The understanding that traumatic past life experiences can have a profound effect on our present life can lead to current life healing. By exploring and confronting the past lives that have created these problems, we can heal the traumas and move on.

Past life experiences are always valuable: whether the memory was pleasant or unpleasant, vivid or vague, there is always something to learn from it. Sometimes the lesson is glaringly obvious and you make instant connections and realisation with an: "Oh! So that's why I've always done/thought that!" Sometimes the lessons are so fleeting they have you frowning in confusion, and understanding gradually seeps into the conscious mind. Maybe some of the lessons to be learned are spread over several lifetimes and our task is to find the missing pieces. Finding these pieces of our cosmic jigsaw can be a fascinating and rewarding pursuit and the lesson itself a deeply profound journey of self-discovery.

All over the world, people are experiencing the amazing benefits that exploring old past life memories and feelings are releasing. During my research I have discovered seemingly incredible recoveries taking place, from long-term physical injuries being resolved, to damaging and limiting self-beliefs being healed, and all this from accessing memories of past lives and healing the trauma.

I accept that many people are sceptical as to whether the images that people recall are actual past lives, or imaginary scenes that the unconscious has created in order to help resolve the issues concerned. I will say a couple of things about my experiences of past life memories, both as an explorer and as a Past Life Therapist.

Firstly if healing, whether physical or emotional occurs after such a therapy session, does it *really* matter if the experience was a real past life memory, or a very imaginative episode of the unconscious mind? Surely the fact that the issues have been resolved is enough? However, those who have gained the benefits through past life regression are in no doubt of their validity.

If however, the unconscious imagination was solely responsible, how can it come up with names, dates, and historically accurate yet obscure information that can later be confirmed? Some people believe that we absorb information from films and studies from childhood through to adulthood, and that this stored but long forgotten information is responsible for 'past life' memories.

Although absorption of information in this way is certainly natural, I believe that given the choice the unconscious would not always choose such unpleasant memories, as you will read within this book.

Mankind's worst enemy is his ego, yet here you will find no Caesar, no Cleopatra and no Romeo and Juliet. You will however read about the experiences of an 18th century sailor, a 17th century nun, an African healer, a Viking warrior and other fascinating people. The imagination alone has limited power to merely 'create' the kind of healing that you will read about.

But the one thing that stands out very clearly from those people who have experienced a past life regression is that in my experience, without exception, they are no longer afraid of dying. This one factor alone is not satisfactorily explained by the sceptics. This lack of fear is a fascinating and rewarding by-product if you like, of the past life experience. No amount of unconscious 'imagining' can so easily dispel such a deep-rooted universal fear. Of all the fears of Mankind, dying is surely the biggest and yet for those who have recalled past life memories this fear has been removed: it no longer concerns them, because they know that death is just part of the spiral of life, of time.

Personally I do believe in past lives: as a therapist I have seen, heard and experienced too much to deny the eternal existence of the soul and of reincarnation. I do not belong to any particular religion, but I am a deeply spiritual person seeking what all religions seek: spiritual enlightenment.

As a holistic therapist and trained hypnotherapist I have helped people resolve deep-rooted issues by using past life therapy when no other avenues of 'traditional' therapy produced results. I have always been open to past life regression on a personal level, but many people aren't. When I started in practice I would offer it as a 'last resort' to clients who weren't responding to hypnosis and I was amazed at the effect that one session could produce. From then on I offered past life regression therapy as a separate therapy of equal importance to my hypnosis practice. On two occasions I have experienced clients who have been very religious, who spontaneously regressed to a past life during a straightforward hypnosis session for problems of a different nature. In both instances the client and I were looking to discover the root cause and whoosh!.... in each case a past life presented itself that created the original problem. The difficulty here was that neither clients' religious teachings nor upbringings accepted reincarnation. Sadly one client dismissed the entire episode and refused to accept the information being shown to her. The other client, a parish vicar, was temporarily astounded before declaring, "God has sent me this memory as a reminder." The knowledge of this new dimension to his past history didn't affect his religious beliefs, or vice versa.

Certain issues respond far better to past life regression therapy including weight loss, serious relationship issues, and fears and phobias, than to more traditional methods of psychoanalysis and counselling.

PHYSICAL & EMOTIONAL HEALING

In some circumstances past life regression has successfully healed long-term physical and psychological ailments, but I would emphasise that in the first instance all physical problems are properly diagnosed by an appropriately qualified healthcare professional. I feel that in some cases conventional methods should be given an opportunity to solve the problem, although it has to be said that a lot of western medicine will ease the symptoms but not cure the *dis-ease*, adding to this the problem that many prescribed chemical drugs create their own unwanted side effects. It is never wise to ignore physical symptoms, and even if you do not wish to have conventional therapy, I believe it is essential to have a professional diagnosis and listen to the options available to you before making a decision.

Every individual has a moral obligation to himself or herself to procure the best treatment available, which suits their individual needs. This could be conventional medicine, holistic therapy, herbalism or any other complementary therapies.

If a past life is genuinely at the root of the problem, then conventional methods of treatment will not heal it; only offer relief to the symptoms. If it sounds like I am trying to deter you from exploring past lives as a possible cause of your illness; I am not. But health is the most important thing you can have, and it would be a dreadful tragedy if you exacerbated the problem because you refused to look at conventional treatments.

Suspected serious illnesses such as cancer and Aids/HIV are always best diagnosed conventionally, and great consideration taken when deciding which route to take for treatment. There is no reason why you cannot use alternative therapy or past life therapy in conjunction with conventional medicine. Past life therapy certainly won't aggravate the condition and may well significantly help. Bear in mind that your therapist will probably wish to communicate with your healthcare professional, and vice versa. This is for your benefit.

So remember: if the problem isn't caused by a past life, then regression won't heal it!

Certain issues may need more than one session to fully understand and resolve the past life to a complete resolution. For anyone who is considering a past life regression there are several important questions that you should ask yourself.

What do I hope to gain from this experience?

If the problem is physical: have I considered all conventional and alternative methods advised by my healthcare professional?

If not, am I putting my health at risk by putting off any treatment?

If the issue is not physical: am I expecting an immediate resolution to the problem, or am I happy to wait and see what happens?

Am I prepared to commit to further sessions if I need them?

Am I seeking a resolution, or am I just looking to understand more about myself?

It is important to know the answers to your questions so you have a clear idea in your mind of what you want to achieve. Be aware that sometimes the presenting problem is not what comes up in a past life regression and that it may take two or three past lives to fully uncover some issues. The best way to explain this is to give an example.

HEALING THE MIND – JUNE'S STORY

June came to see me about a weight loss problem that she had been unable to sort out herself, or with the help of her GP. Over the past five years she had tried numerous diets, slimming clubs, purchased expensive gym memberships, special dietary foods and even 'quick' weight loss tablets. Her GP had finally told her that the only other option was to consider having her stomach stapled. June was horrified and, like me, did not believe that such a drastic method could be the only solution.

Over those five years however, she had identified her binge 'triggers' and several other important factors that had led her to believe that her problem may stem from a past life experience:

June had always had a problem with food. She hadn't always been fat, but she had always felt uncomfortable around food. She recalled under hypnosis, that at the age of 3 she went to her first birthday party. She was naturally very excited as she was looking forward to playing games and all the other things you do at a child's party.

However, she also recalled that when she arrived at her friend's house, she saw the table groaning under the weight of party food. She connected with the feelings that image evoked and found that fear and obsession was stronger than the feeling of excitement. June remembered that for the duration of the party, until teatime, she was obsessed with getting to the table of food before it was gone. She remembered being afraid that she would get there last and that there would be no food left for her. She even recalled 'planning' a route to the chair that was nearest to her so she could climb up to the table before everyone else.

This is highly unusual activity for a weight loss client. The majority of women are emotional eaters, or have put on weight since having children. But June had always shown different behaviour around food. When she spoke to her mother about the memory of the party, her mother remembered it at once. She said how odd it had been that June was so excited before she arrived, and once there could barely take her eyes off the food long enough to play a game.

The fact that June had previously sought the help of a hypnotherapist to overcome her problem and was unsuccessful was also highly significant. Hypnosis is usually a highly successful solution for people wanting to gain control over their eating habits. This pointed June in the direction of a past life. June came to me specifically to discover and resolve the past life that had created difficulties for her with food in this lifetime.

However, what came up in the following 2-hour session was not exactly what she had expected! Sometimes, no matter what you intend to discover your unconscious decides you need to see something else. In her session June experienced three past lives but only one was directly linked to past lives concerning food. In the first she was a victim of the Irish potato famine and saw her family die due to lack of food, before succumbing herself. The lesson she learned from that life was: 'There will never be enough food!'

In the second past life issues of obsession came up as June lost her husband to another, younger woman as a result of her reluctance as a 'lady', not to fight for him or to make a fuss. She died alone and sad. The lesson she learned from that life was: 'You have to take what you want before someone else takes it.' In the third and final past life there was little visual information, but very strong sensations of 'You must get what you need when it's available.' June 'felt' rather than saw anything in this experience but she said the feeling of being deprived was very strong. Like the second lifetime, this wasn't directly related to food, but all three lifetimes were linked by a common thread. All three lessons together created a problem that connected itself to food (the lack of which had previously caused her death) in this lifetime:

'There will never be enough food!'

'You have to take what you want, before someone else takes it.'

'You must get what you need when it's available.'

Even though now in England there is no shortage of food (in fact there is too much), the three lessons had been attached to such suffering and painful experiences in those past lives that they had carried forward into this lifetime.

It is these lessons, and sometimes promises made in past lives that create problems in the present.

We worked with each lifetime putting the lessons and experiences into perspective, cutting the ties with the emotional attachments she had made with food, and resolving each lifetime as they linked together. June was finally able to release the old obsession and fears she had carried forward to this lifetime. She lost four stone in 14 months and now has no problem staying slim and healthy.

Her obsessions for food have disappeared.

The point of this example is to demonstrate that you cannot always tell what past life memories will surface even if like June, you have very specific ideas of what you want to solve.

So why do it?

Because whatever past life memory you access it will tell you something that you need to know. There will always be a connection, and you will always have a better understanding of who you are, and why you are the way you are. That past life memory may spontaneously lead to recalling another past life memory. You may need to recall a certain sequence to get the healing you need. Your unconscious mind will always show you what it believes you need to know in order to make healing connections and to resolve conflicts. Often the processing and understanding of information can take a couple of days.

Some problems like June's have accumulated over several lifetimes. With a good therapist and 2-3 hours, you should be able to access several past lives and resolve those problems, although you must be willing to do more sessions if you want to get the resolution to more serious issues. The ease with which you can enter your past lives will increase with experience.

HEALING THE BODY

Past life wounds or illnesses can be remembered on a cellular as well as soul level, and symptoms or marks can occur on the body in the current life. There are numerous theories as to why this happens but no one accepted explanation. As fears and other emotions can have a psychological effect on the current life, it seems logical that the injuries and in particular the cause of death, can affect the body in much the same way. In the case of wounds, violent or unexpected death, or painful illness the side effects on the current life are often physical and emotional. Recurring symptoms in the current life can often correlate to the age of the original injury or wound in the past life. Recurring symptoms are often your body's way of telling you that you need to look to a deeper, psychological explanation.

The following table shows examples of possible effects in the current life of past life physical trauma. Both the physical effects and the emotional counterparts are shown.

Physical symptoms in current life	Past life cause	Emotional effect
Headaches/pain.	Head wounds, madness. Hanging, strangulation.	Tenseness, disorientation.
Throat problems, laryngitis.	Strangulation, hanging. Killed for your beliefs.	Fear of speaking your mind, timidity, poor communication skills, 'doormat' syndrome.
Chest problems, asthma.	Crushed, suffocation, drowning.	Anger or frustration, Feelings of being over-whelmed.
Stomach ulcers, mouth ulcers, indigestion.	Wounds by stabbing or shooting. Death by poisoning.	Sick of life, vulnerable,

Back pain, spinal problems.	Wounds by stabbing or shooting. Death by injury. Disability.	Lack of trust, shock: 'stabbed in the back.' Weak personality –'spineless.'
Uterus, menstrual or fertility problems.	Dying in childbirth, injuries cased by rape or abuse, death wounds.	Dislike of, or obsession with children, fear of pregnancy.
Leg pains, disability, gout.	Amputations, accidents, paralysis. Wounds or injury to legs.	Anger, helplessness, resentment. Fear of life.
Arthritis.	Injury in specific joints, rigid lifestyles, hard physical life. Amputations.	Rigidity of thought or opinions, hard-heartedness.
Anxiety attacks & phobias.	Death experiences, fearful lives, persecution.	Anxiety unrelated to present life events.
Scars, birthmarks.	Wounds, injuries.	Self-consciousness.
Psoriasis, eczema.	Wounds, pain, injuries.	Self-consciousness, irritation, depression.

This table represents a small sample of the cause and affect that symptoms of past life incidents can have on the present life. It gives you an idea of just how deeply past lives can affect you now. Remember that any pain should be correctly diagnosed by a qualified healthcare professional, so you know what you are treating. Past life therapy cannot adversely affect any conventional treatment you are receiving so there is no reason you cannot undergo both if you wish.

Indicators that a past life may be the root cause of present physical problems include pain or other symptoms that come and go at certain times: under stress, when dealing with one particular person, at certain times of the year. Kinds of intermittent pain may be related to certain times of the year for example, a back injury that reoccurs in summer/autumn, may relate to an injury sustained in a past life during harvesting. Pain or discomfort experienced when you have contact with one specific person could be related to a past life where that person was in a conflict situation with you. In these instances it is possible to experience spontaneous flashback images when you meet someone with whom you have had a strong positive, or negative, past life connection. These indicators are reminders of that past event or conflict that need healing.

Even if your injury has been caused by an accident or has been exacerbated by a series of accidents or events in this life, the original weakness can often be traced back to a past life. Once that past life has been recalled and healed, then the fundamental weakness will be resolved. This often leads to an increase of strength in the damaged area, and any future treatments will now be more successful.

I had a car accident when I was 16, which led to several years of tremendous pain in my neck, and to a much lesser degree, my back. Traditional treatment alleviated the pain, but the problem never really healed. At a workshop I recalled a past life where I had received a blow to the back of the neck, exactly where my current pain was, and after the regression I noticed a distinct improvement in my mobility and my pain relief. Years later I was involved in another accident, which exacerbated my lower back problem, and in the last two years, I have had two further incidences or 'triggers', that left me further debilitated.

The first happened when I damaged my back last year in the garden and, this May, when I had just recovered from that incident, I did it again. I couldn't believe it! This last event was much worse than the previous injury – I was confined to bed for a week in agonising pain. I asked myself what was going on. It seemed that my body's reaction to the incident was excessive in relation to what had happened, despite the previous weakness. I began to wonder if my body was trying to tell me something.

Being incapacitated has given me plenty of time on my hands to reflect and has prompted me to write this book: something I have been intending to do for a couple of years but put off, as I am a great procrastinator. It is as if I have finally been forced to stop and write this book now. Perhaps my receiving this injury was the only way to ensure that I got on with it?

I have had plenty of time to think during my incapacitation and it has recently occurred to me, that in several of my past lives I have sustained injuries to my back when I was in my 30's. I was either injured, or I died. As I have just passed 38, I wondered if this is a connection. That I have had several problems in the last few years, points to an accumulation of past life traumas that are affecting me at this particular time in my current life. I am still working on this past life connection as I write this book.

Often, when an increase in the number of physical problems occurs in a limited time span, it is a message from your subconscious urging you to stop and take a closer look at something. Your mind continually communicates to you through your body, but in this era of increased stress and responsibility we rarely stop to listen. This results in an increase of mental and physical *dis*-ease, which in turn results in disease.

I was diagnosed as having a prolapsed disc and damaged nerve, which disabled me to the degree that all I could do for several weeks was lie down, and I experienced constant pain. I was on several drugs for pain and to help me relax, which seemed to make little difference other than to make me physically sick. After a few weeks I felt that I needed to gain control of the situation. I took myself off the medicines and started a course of accupuncture. The change was almost immediate: my depression lifted, my mind felt clearer and more alert, the pain was manageable. My mobility was still seriously restricted and the pain was ever present, but I felt different. For the first time in several weeks I felt able to do something, so I started this book. Daily I reflected on the past lives that held memories of injuries sustained to my back, and worked on using self-hypnosis and healing visualisations to ease the pain, heal the inflammation in the disc and give strength to the supporting muscles. I found that my visualisations were most effective during my acupuncture sessions and that as I meditated, I automatically made spiritual connections. Mr Ding, my acupuncturist, said that I was 'cold and damp' inside, and I took the opportunity to meditate on that during my session. I connected with the past life in this book 'The Alcoholic' and felt that this cold feeling related to that past life experience. The injury was in the spinal area opposite the solar plexus where, in that incarnation, I had held feelings of fear and guilt 'like a cold, hard ball.' This connection was too intense to be a coincidence.

I eventually connected that feeling with the fear and by doing a visualisation where I visited my internal solar plexus, I found a cave that was indeed cold and damp – there should have been a fire within the centre – the creative fire, but it was no more than glowing embers. My creative fire was almost extinguished and the fear was allowed to grow. Over the next few weeks I regularly visualised visiting that cave every day: stoking up the fire, heaping logs up against the cave wall to provide a continuous supply of fuel and watching the heat dry out the cave and melt the hard, cold, ball of ice that represented the fear that I had carried around since the 'Alcoholic' reincarnation. I visualised this icy ball sitting on a grate, so that when it melted it would drain away, and out of the cave (out of me). This whole experience has been a profound one and I continue to make progress every day.

I use these creative visualisation techniques with my past life clients as they are extremely powerful. Given the opportunity the human body is more than capable of healing itself. Sometimes it needs a kick-start to initiate the process.

CHAPTER TWO

'THE ALCOHOLIC'

(Training workshop regression – volunteer guinea pig!
– with Dominic Beirne & Steve Burgess)

Deborah's experience

"Recalling past lives is comforting –
I know that I can come back to correct my mistakes"

CH

"I wanted to access a past life to gain knowledge about any problems that may be holding me back now. I have always been interested in regression and strongly believe that it holds the key to understanding ourselves." Deborah

THE ALCOHOLIC

I am a man, about 35 years old. I'm big and strong and quite tall. It is about 1730. I am wearing a dull white, loose shirt, brown breeches and boots. I'm a bit scruffy but not dirty. I have long, dark hair, tied back into a ponytail. When I was in the tunnel approaching this past life I could hear the sound of my friends laughing, as I went towards them. I felt happy and excited to see them. I knew they were in the inn and they were a raucous crowd. But when I enter the inn, everything is quiet. It is very dark. I am standing in the main room of the inn.

It is barely lit by the dirty window and a couple of candles on the tables. I feel confused. It takes me a while to focus on the room around me and I feel very anxious and afraid. It is almost as if everyone had just upped and left a few seconds before I arrived. People's belongings are still on the tables: ale half drunk, a pipe left on the table etc. I can hear my heart thumping in my chest. I become aware that I am supposed to be meeting four of my friends here, but I am also aware that I am a bit late. We meet here regularly but I have a feeling of doom. It takes me a while to link into the feelings and I realise that we have been meeting in secret in a room at the back of the inn: we were planning something.

I recall that we are plotting to murder the local landowner, who is also a magistrate. We don't consider it murder really as he is a tyrant. He controls the town and is a nasty man. He fixes trials and many innocent people have been hung. He seems to enjoy terrorising the local people and they are all afraid of him. He doesn't respect the law of the land and does his own thing. The whole town lives in terror. We had been planning for weeks to kill him. I am worried about my friends, they should be here. The emptiness of the inn is not natural, something is very wrong. I am scared they have been caught. I am covered in a cold sweat and gripped by panic. I knew I should be out looking for my friends but I am too scared. I can't physically leave the inn. I feel stuck here, rigid with fear, for ages.

Next I am in a crowd of people at the town square. I am shaking with fear and still covered from head to toe with a cold sweat. I have never been so terrified. I know that my friends have been caught and that this is a public hanging. I know that there should have been a trial, but there hasn't been. As I am part of the group, I know that had I met them on time, I too would have been caught. I should have been caught, but I am still free. I feel guilty, but there is nothing I can do.

I am so scared that I will give myself away, or that I too will be caught and hung. I don't want to be here, but I cannot move away. I don't understand: who would have betrayed us?

I push my way through the crowd to the middle, near the scaffold, but not near enough for my friends to see me. I can see the scaffold: there are four nooses hanging down. I feel sick with terror. The people in the crowd around me are angry: they are screaming and shouting, I cannot hear clearly.

There is a disturbance to the left of the scaffold and the crowd parts: I see a cart making its way to the steps of the scaffold. My friends are tied to the cart, their hands are tied behind their backs and they are blindfolded. Oh my relief! And such guilt for feeling relief! They cannot see me and therefore point me out for capture. I am still afraid that they may have named me as an accomplice. They are taken off the cart and put struggling into the nooses. The crowd is furious, and my friends are shouting into the crowd, inciting them I think. I can't make out what anyone is saying I can just hear the din.

The crowd is angry at what is happening to my friends. I tear myself away from the town square and run through the town, which is deserted. I am distraught and I run away from the town, eventually I collapse at last in a cornfield, where I am crying and shaking.

Time passes, but I am not sure how much. I know that my friends are now dead.

I move forward in time to find myself at the port. I board a ship and work for my passage. I load and unload the cargo, mainly sacks of grain and barrels. I can still feel the pain, shock and grief like a cold, hard, black ball in my solar plexus.

I move forward again. I am in a foreign port. I am now strong, suntanned and very muscular. I feel nothing: I am neither happy nor content but still working on the ships. I still feel the hard ball of pain and guilt.

Now I am on an island. It is a beautiful, peaceful place: the sea is a translucent blue/green, and the sand is white. I think I am in Jamaica or one of the islands on the silk trading route. It is wonderfully hot. I have earned good money over the years and have spent little on myself, but I am wearing new, clean clothes. Ships still come to the port to trade, but I no longer work on them. I just buy rum and brandy by the barrel. I drink a lot. I have built myself a big grass hut. There are natives living on the island, but I keep myself to myself. We live side by side but are not friendly.

I am older now, about 55. I am now in a much smaller mud and grass hut, which is very squalid. I can hear flies buzzing around me: they annoy me but I do nothing about them. I feel old, tired and very dirty. I do nothing but drink – I am an alcoholic. I am lying on my back on the floor in a drunken stupor. I have nothing left – no money. I am trying to bury the pain and the guilt in drink. I am alone. I used to shout and throw bottles at the natives if they came near me and now they no longer do.

The day I die I am lying in my hut. I cannot move. I have had a hangover for years. My mouth is dry. I can feel that I am slipping away bit by bit. I can feel my brain shutting down little by little and the numbness consumes my body. It is like gradually shutting every cell down, one by one. I feel my life slowly slipping away and it is not nice: I am aware of it, but I don't care.

HEALING OUTCOMES

Looking at the whole story and the relevance it had to my current life was fascinating. I was amazed. Alcohol had always been a big part of my life: I had always enjoyed a good drinking session, but always felt guilty for drinking. Binge drinking and drinking alone had always been how I preferred to drink, although I mainly drank in company. Throughout my adult life I was a heavy drinker, and after my divorce, I drank alone more than with friends. I had reached a point where I was concerned about the quantities of cider and wine I was drinking, but didn't consider that I had a problem. Perhaps this was because I always (mistakenly) associated alcoholics with being spirit drinkers.

Guilt was something I remember feeling as a small child, even when I had done nothing wrong. If anyone were apportioning blame for example at school, I would always feel guilty, panicky and afraid, even when I was innocent.

It is also very odd how this experience unlocked forgotten feelings and memories from childhood. Like the time I won a bottle of sloe gin at a village fayre when I was ten. I recalled anticipating the flavour of alcohol, even before I drank it, and the urgency of wanting to drink it. So much so, that I hid in the garden and drunk the bottle in one go, it was horrendous, but I drank it anyway. This was my first alcoholic drink. I also recalled when I was about 13, clearing up the dregs of various bottles in my parent's drinks cabinet.

I have always loved the sea and ships and I whenever I see films set in that period, I feel a deep sense of loss and regret for that life. It was a hard but simple life in a beautiful land and I miss the relative freedom of it. I miss the life on the sea and travelling to different countries.

At the end of the session, my colleague and I worked on healing and releasing the 'cold, hard black ball' that I had carried around since that incarnation. I dissolved most of it, but for some reason I felt the need to hold onto a little of it 'as a reminder'. At the time

I wasn't sure why but looking at the situation retrospectively, I realise that as I was in the regression, a part of me understood that this was going to change my life. I think I needed to retain part of it as a reminder not to slip back into my old drinking habits. I needn't have worried: I didn't touch alcohol for two years, and I now feel safe enough to have the very occasional alcoholic drink.

But the truly amazing thing was that from the moment I woke up from that regression all desire for alcohol disappeared. I don't even think about it and I don't miss it. I have discovered that I do not need it for confidence, comfort or to have fun with my friends.

Deborah

ANALYSIS

These previous beliefs were literally a 'hangover' from that previous lifetime. This experience has strengthened my belief in myself and has also changed my life on a physical level. The ability for this kind of healing is typical of past life regression therapy.

It is a very liberating and powerful experience to overcome a long-term dependency, even one that you don't recognise at the time. All it took was one regression to tell me that I had already wasted one lifetime through drinking and that I didn't need to do it again. It was an old need, and I could let it go.

STYLE

This regression was guided by a professional colleague at a training workshop. I was the volunteer guinea pig! Initially I felt self-conscious, which has always been an issue itself and was one reason that I forced myself to volunteer. I quickly found myself in a light state of relaxation, vividly recalling the terror and anxiety of this lifetime. Although I was not deeply regressed, I was able to recall clearly and in great detail, the colours and descriptions of the past life. The feeling of fear and terror was like nothing I have ever experienced.

I was also aware of my other colleagues in the room with me, and the noises they made. This was a fascinating experience as I felt that my consciousness was 'split', between two places. This particular experience was also interesting as it showed me that a deep level of hypnosis or altered state was not essential for recalling past life memories.

CHAPTER THREE

'VIKING HATRED'

Uma's experience

"Life and death are entwined
like a rose around an arbour"

NH

"I had a flash of understanding that this Viking had been still so much alive in me for nearly 35 years, that he'd prevented me from completely integrating my female body in this current incarnation." Uma

VIKING HATRED

I used a shamanic plant called ayahuasca, during a session in the rain forest, in Central America.

My only intention was healing and I fully trusted the brew, the place where it happened and the shamans involved. Thus, healing did happen and more than once.

A past life came into my awareness on this occasion: I became aware that I was a man. I was able to compare the energies that I was feeling as a man to those that I was familiar with as a woman. The male energies were (as I defined them) cold, hard and full – compared to warm, soft and empty as a female. These emotions were all located in the stomach area.

Then I went deeper into this man that I'd become and I knew that I was a Viking warrior.

I remembered my face and the shape of my body (there were no visions involved, I was just feeling the memories) and then as I went deeper I remembered my personality. I especially remember the anger and hatred for women: that was the point for my whole healing. This Viking man was obviously a raider, a rapist and a killer. Not a nice person at all. This hatred for women was deep.

Going deeper into his psyche I found an intense longing for the 'perfect woman', the one of his dreams that he'd never found. Through his longing I felt intense compassion for his wound: the hatred, the killings, and suddenly a thought came to me exactly as this: "but...I am the woman I've been looking for all this time!" That is: me here and now! I had a flash of understanding that this Viking had been still so much alive in me for nearly 35 years, that he'd prevented me from completely integrating my female body in this current incarnation, which suddenly explained my hatred for it, and my long-term desire to be a man. And healing simply happened through this awareness, compassion and understanding!

I was able to release the Viking in me by simply putting to rest his unconscious search for the 'perfect woman', and fulfilling this secret desire by integrating my female body with love for the first time in my life.

HEALING OUTCOMES

I spent the next few hours in wonder for being a woman, and my whole life gradually changed since:

I started appreciating baking, normal 'woman tasks', and became closer and closer to the Earth.

I had been floating on a cloud for many years with a kind of fear of the Earth, now I cannot even sleep in a house – I live in a yurt in a field!

Uma

ANALYSIS

This experience was an amazing insight into the extreme difference between the male and female psyche. Uma was able to easily clarify the emotions attached to this Viking warrior – the hatred, the feeling of cold, hardness and being full of that hatred and violent energy. Clearly this warrior hated his violent life but his deep loneliness and longing for that ideal female companion that existed only in his imagination drove him to further atrocities.

STYLE

As I mention in Chapter Thirteen, indigenous herbs can be used to alter your states of consciousness as Uma did, but this experience was in context of the time, place and culture with which she found herself. Uma's intent was deeply spiritual and not just a physical need to get high.

CHAPTER FOUR

'EMILY AND HER LOST LOVE'

(One to one hypnotherapy)

H.G.'s experience

*"Birth and death are doorways
to the experiences between"*

NH

"I had read several books on reincarnation and hypnosis and was very interested to try and experience a regression for myself." HG

EMILY AND HER LOST LOVE

It's about 1800. My name is Emily (Mutton?) I am about 8 years old. I am dressed in a black, calf length dress, with black boots and a brown shawl. I am standing in front of huge, closed, wrought iron gates. They have a round, twisted metal handle. I am pressing my face against the bars; I can see a long yellow gravel driveway leading up to a house. I am feeling anxious. I have a brown leather bag with me containing my meagre belongings. I am being sent from my home where I live with my mother and baby brother to work at the big house, 'Grovelands', in Kent. (I kept saying to myself what a silly name that was.)

The house belongs to Sir (?) Alfred and Lady Mary Beaufort (Or Beaumont?) I had no idea about the arrangements for my future. All I knew was that I had to see the cook and I didn't know when or if, I'd be going home again. I lifted up my hand to open the gate and I saw my tiny hand with the nails bitten down: I was too scared to open the gate. I wasn't sad about leaving my mum – she was nice enough but very stressed. As I recalled her I saw she was plain looking with light brown hair tied up in a bun. She was by the fireplace in the kitchen. The baby's cot was nearby. I knew I had to go away: Mum needed the money although it wasn't going to be a lot. I was going into service early. I should have been 12.

I only saw the cook and one other servant whilst I was there: it was a small household. Occasionally I glimpsed Sir & Lady Beaufort. He was retired from the army where he had risen quite high.

Then I was about 14/15, I was in my attic room. I had just washed my hair, which was long and thin. I was content. It was winter and I think we were in Bath. There were only about five other servants in the house at this time. Work was ok, I no longer did the dishes or prepared the vegetables: I was mainly sewing and mending. Lady Beaufort had discovered that I sewed well: she liked my neat tiny stitches, so mostly I was asked to mend things and embroider for her. I was training to be a seamstress.

I helped to serve the food occasionally when they were entertaining.

Then I was about 23. I was standing outside the door of my cottage, with my son of about 18 months old. I had married a man called Mark Taylor. He was a garden landscaper and designer. He worked for Sir Alfred and others as well: he designed gardens in Kent. The cottage was lovely and I was very happy. Mark was a wonderful, beautiful man: tall, blonde and strong: my soul mate.

We had our own home that I think was within the grounds of the Beauforts' estate, but we paid no rent. It wasn't a tied cottage. I occasionally did some embroidery but it wasn't a job, more as a favour.

I got the feeling that Lady Beaufont was very fond of me: I had been with her since I was a young girl.

Forward to when I was about 43. I was plumper now, wearing a brown dress with a white lace collar. I was sad and terribly lonely. Mark had died about ten years ago (so we'd been married for about ten years).

My son had also died as a toddler, but I was more upset about my husband dying as we had had a wonderful relationship. My husband had died whilst planning a garden design for someone local. He had wanted to design a man-made lake of gigantic proportions, with an island where he planned to build a summerhouse. I remember discussing my fear with him: I just hadn't felt it was a good idea but he was very enthusiastic and creative. One day he and his client were on the existing lake that Mark wanted to extend: the boat capsized and he drowned.

I went forward to the day I died. I was old, with white hair and shrivelled skin. I was sitting in a kind of deckchair. I was wearing a flowery dress and I was ready to go. I felt very tired. I had never married again, although I had stayed in our house. Mark's death had just devastated me: I had lost my best friend, my husband and my lover.

HEALING OUTCOMES

My lesson to pass on was that I don't have to be alone for the rest of my life. I was being shown that I had had a lifetime of experiencing the loss of a husband and of shutting myself away. I had basically just waited thirty years to die. I was telling myself not to be alone forever. This was after my marriage of ten years had broken down, and at a time when I felt that I would be alone for the rest of my life. But I was ok with that in this lifetime, as I enjoy my own company. Perhaps this past life was warning me how easy it would be for me to stay alone, so should make a point of not being so, as I had experienced that already?

The relationship that I had had in that lifetime with my husband Mark was extraordinary: I haven't felt that in this lifetime with any of my partners, or my husband. But as soon as I experienced that relationship as Emily, I instantly recognised it as what I have been searching for in this lifetime with every relationship I have entered into. It was like recognition of the perfect relationship. I realised that what I had been searching for in my past relationships was real, not just an adolescent romantic ideal. I wonder still if I will ever have that again.

H.G.

ANALYSIS

H.G. remembered so well the feeling as that little girl of the fear of having to leave home so young and go to work for strangers. Also though a sense of maturity, a knowing that that was how it was, and there was no other option. She never recalled going back home but knew that she did see her mother and brother again. The Beaufort's (or Beaumont's – it was not quite clear) were very kind people and treated her well. This feeling of being alone for ever was not just connected to the breakdown of H.G.'s marriage in this lifetime: she had always been a bit hermit-like and comfortable with her own company. H.G. has had several lifetimes of being alone, but this lifetime particularly illustrated the loneliness aspect of being without a loving partner.

H.G. felt that she had wasted the remaining years after being widowed, by being miserable and sad.

She never made any attempt to find someone else and 'hid' in her cottage: dependent on the embroidery work from the big house.

H.G. feels that part of the message was that although she might never have had the wonderful relationship experienced with her husband, she could still have been happy again, but *chose* not to be. The lesson was that in her current lifetime she could choose *not* to be alone as it isn't necessary.

H.G. also identified her husband in that lifetime as someone she knows well in this lifetime.

"I recognised him several years after this regression, and it came as quite a shock. He has been in many dreams and past lives with me, and is indeed a soul mate."

STYLE

This regression was as a one to one hypnotherapy session. The benefit of hypnosis is that specific details are recalled easily and you can often recall names and places clearly. Even details such as the laces on her boots and the gravel of the driveway, was visually as clear as if she was standing there now. Hypnosis allows a deeply relaxed state during a regression, and frequently the emotions, in this case particularly the feelings of love for her husband, and then the loneliness and unhappiness of leading a widow's life, are profound.

CHAPTER FIVE

'THE AMERICAN DREAM'

(Spontaneous dream recall)

Amanda's experience

*"Life is a journey to which
there is no final destination"*

CH

"My interest in past lives lies in the spontaneous dreams and experiences that help to make sense of my current life. As a healer and counsellor my own therapeutic journey has sometimes included information (as in this dream), which confirms to me its validity and the healing it can bring in the present. Like shadows being dispelled in the light of self knowledge." Amanda

THE AMERICAN DREAM

DREAM BACKGROUND

I am in an American Burger Bar. It is a modern building, but stands alone in the wilderness of mid-west America. The dream is full of colour: alive and vibrant. The burger bar staff are busy serving customers. Someone is with me. I know they are there and even though I can't see them, I sense them to my left and slightly behind me. The events that follow are shown to me at my guide's direction.

THE DREAM

There is a hum of activity in the place. Everything seems normal, but then at an unspoken signal from my guide, we lift off the ground and fly out of the building through the door as someone else comes in. At the speed of thought, we fly high over the landscape. Everything is bathed in sunlight and warmth. The land is green and verdant. We seem to be rushing toward something and I feel expectant, curious and nervous. Everything I experience is from this bird's eye view.

Ahead of us I see a tall man wearing a chequered shirt and jeans. His hair is reddish brown. He walks slowly: relaxed and happy with his arm over the shoulder of a young boy who's about

9-12 years old. Father and son in company together: all is well with them and I sense they are talking about easy things.

In the next moment, again at some unspoken signal from my guiding companion, we are flying at a tremendous speed back down the track from where the man and boy have come. The landscape rushes past below us and after a few hundred yards we come hovering to a halt. There is a band of Indian Braves (Mohicans I think), on horseback. They seem to be in a hurry and with purpose they are galloping in the direction of the man and the boy.

I am feeling very anxious and fearful. As the braves pass below us we wheel around and again, speed toward the man and boy ahead of the braves. My heart is beating very fast and I know something awful is going to happen. When we reach the two, they are still walking along and seem unaware of the danger they are in.

My guide and I hover above the scene and almost immediately the braves are upon the man and boy. The braves are whooping and making a high pitched hunting noise in their throats, which breaks the peaceful silence of before.

They circle around and close in on the father and son. Two of the braves grab the boy and hold him by the arms. They force him to watch as the others take hold of his father.

The braves, holding the man, put some sort of contraption on his body and literally break him into two. As this happens I hear him scream, feel his fear and the desperation inside him for his son. I scream out to my guide "No!" in a long drawn out cry and curl into a foetal ball in mid air. Next they scalp him with blunt and bloody instruments. Every action they take is done in a brutal, triumphant manner and they make the boy watch as they display his father's scalp.

(At this point I am in a state of high anxiety in the dream and feel panic in my whole body. I say to my guide that we should help them, but I am told just to watch. We are the observers and not participants of what unfolds. At this point my guide is on my right though still out of sight.)

All of this happened in what seems like only moments. My understanding of the events: the whole of it and its reasoning, are as instantaneous as thought. I understood their intention to make a show of killing the man while his son watched. They wanted to create fear in the white man. They wanted the son to witness, feel fear and hate them because they knew that the hatred and fear the boy would carry with him was a continuation of their single, violent act. Because of this, the revenge that they took on this one white man would live on in the boy and be told to others, who would also fear and hate. This is their revenge.

I felt the grief and sorrow of the man that his son was made to watch, that his wife would never see him again, that mother and son were now alone without him and would have to go on living. He understood all of this, and now I understood also.

The dream then moved on. The braves released the boy and left the man's broken body on the ground. They mounted their ponies and raced off, now silent but holding the scalp up high.

Next thing I am aware of is that I am at ground level (and alone now) and the modern day customers from the burger bar are carrying the man's body aloft, toward the building of the modern day. They are going to take him inside. I can see surrounding his body a host of bee people. They are large and a shiny, nutty brown colour with human faces: round and chubby like children's. They are concentrating all their efforts to sting him. I know that the stings are healing stings but no matter how they strain and concentrate, the man is still dead and nothing can be done to bring him back to life. They are deeply sad and I can feel all this, understand and know all this. He is carried inside and the dream ends here.

HEALING OUTCOMES

It happened at a time in my life when much healing was taking place on many levels: levels that at the time I was not consciously aware of. It was only a part of my healing journey but one that was so vividly experienced. I knew then and know now, that this dream showed my own death experience from a previous life. I can see now the healing that I experienced through it. It was necessary to be in a place of understanding. To remember and acknowledge what happened to me and the legacy it left behind in my family. An individual story and yet also part of a collective experience of that time period in history, which has left a legacy behind it. That understanding: his/my understanding, needed to be brought into the modern day setting (the burger bar). I needed to re-experience my death and what it meant on different levels, to remember my own understanding, to bring it forward and accept that what happened was as part of a larger collective experience. The consequences of which were far reaching, right into the modern day.

That understanding and the healing in my psyche that it has released for me enabled my psyche to let go of carrying the fear, pain and the grief of that whole period as my family experienced it: as the white man experienced it collectively. I hope that my healing added to the collective healing, like a drop of cooling water.

As I see it I was in the burger bar, modern day, without understanding. I then re-experienced my death and the legacy, my grief, fear and sorrow, and brought all this back to the modern day. No amount of effort (bee people) can bring back that life, that body, but the understanding can be brought back to the modern day: this life, here and now. And I feel peace with it.

Amanda

ANALYSIS

This is unusual in that the dream is a 'world level healing' regression. It speaks not only to the person who dreamed it, but also to a whole culture. In this case the white man and the Native American Indian. This is a world healing event, which helps to heal the trauma on a deep spiritual level of many generations on both sides.

Very spiritual people, and those who are undergoing great spiritual learning frequently experience this kind of regression.

Not everyone can recognise an experience for its universal meaning, however Mandy has undertaken much spiritual and holistic work over the years, and this has helped her to see deeper.

STYLE

This regression was a spontaneous dream recall. Immediate connections and understanding occurred as the dream unfolded. This is one of the advantages of spontaneous dream regression: the healing and learning usually occur simultaneously.

People often dream but don't recall them – this is because the processing has occurred automatically and there is no need to remember. When a dream is recalled it is your subconscious reminding you of something or calling your attention to something. Often this means that there is further work to do, or healing to take place. In an experience such as this, it is a reminder of the deep world level healing that is taking place.

The interesting aspect of dream regression is that real life and past life intertwine. In this example the burger bar represented the modern 'doorway' to the past life but also symbolised the modern attitude and state of mind of the dreamer. This mix of metaphorical and symbolic with the divine information is common in dreams. For telling a past life dream from a 'normal' dream see Chapter Thirteen, How to Access Your Past Lives.

CHAPTER SIX

'VICTORIAN CONNECTIONS'

(Mass seminar regression with Denise Linn)

Anon's experience

"Today you are the accumulation of your previous incarnations"

CH

"I went to a huge seminar in London to meet Denise Linn and at the group regression I wanted to find out more about my occasionally difficult relationship with my eldest daughter. We didn't seem to understand each other very well sometimes and I wanted to improve this situation. Regression is something I have always wanted to do, but I didn't want to experience it alone for the first time. A group seminar was ideal for me." Anon.

VICTORIAN CONNECTIONS

My time tunnel started as a glass tube, curving to the right. On each side of me were images of the past, like models posed or life-sized photos on display. These images then sped up past me, making it seem as if I was standing still in the tunnel and the images were moving, whereas really I was moving forward very fast. There was mist at the end of the tunnel. We had to hold in our minds an affirmation to get to the source of a current problem. I chose to look at the difficulty in communication and understanding between my daughter and myself.

1..2..3………………..

I stepped through the mist into a past life.

I am a teenager, 16-18 years old. I am standing in my brown lace up boots (same as the ones that I had bought just before coming to the seminar). They are the 'typical' style of the period in which I find myself. I am standing on a cobbled street. I am dressed in a rough brown dress with white underskirt and white cap. I am carrying a large wicker basket. I am pale with freckles and mousy hair and I am fair looking. I feel calm and in control: I'm not happy, more content. I'm in a busy market place and I'm in a hurry. I am aware that my hands are red and tender, I realise that I am a servant and that I work extremely hard. I get the feeling that lots of floor scrubbing and washing up is involved! I walk through the market and I am aware that I have only bought a few things from the list I have: certainly not enough for my Mistress. I feel that I am being followed.

(This could be awareness of me as an onlooker.)

I passed market stalls without purchasing anything else and

hurried along. I made eye contact with a stallholder in the market that I recognised there, but I can't place him.

I suddenly find myself in another street: I think it is called Wimpole Street. There are tall houses standing on the right hand side of the wide cobbled street, clearly in a better class of area than the market. Each house had four white stone steps leading up to the front door and black railings ran along the front of the houses. On the other side of the street high railings ran along the length of the street with tall gas lamps lining the road. At the near end of the street, the end house was attached to a low red-bricked tunnel: an archway.

I walk up the steps of the house that was about third from the end by the tunnel. I recall thinking that this front door approach was odd for a servant. The lady of the house is very well to do. She is very well dressed and has a hat with feathers in it. I recognised her as my eldest daughter in my current lifetime. She had a go at me as soon as I walked in the door. I was aware that she always took this approach to me no matter what I did, or how hard I worked. Nothing was ever good enough for this woman.

Next I went up to my room that I shared with another servant, whom I recognised as my youngest daughter in this lifetime! She is much the same in character: lively, engaging, good sense of humour. She is very streetwise and knew how things worked. We got on very well and were very close, we talked about our situation and I used to talk about getting out, about doing something else. She couldn't understand this. She had a realist-fatalistic attitude: this is our situation in life, we have to make the best of it and we can't change it.

I discovered that I used to spend my time off, what there was of it, writing mainly poetry but also stories. They were very good and my colleague supported me. I was very insecure and unconfident about my ability. I felt that I did not belong there: there was a feeling that I had fallen on hard times and was forced to get work as a servant. I had a feeling of having lost my former status. Consequently I found it very difficult working for this very demanding woman. One day I was summoned to the drawing room where the lady had my folder of writings. She was angry with me and said she didn't pay me to write, and that they were no more than illiterate babblings. She then threw them on the fire to burn. I felt such a rage boil up inside me that I instantly recognised. I hated and resented her so much, she was pure nastiness. I felt that something awful was about to happen.

I then moved forward to the day I died. I was old and wearing a brown dress. I was in bed, just slipping away. My friend was at my side. I was surprised that I was in the attic room, poor. I died peacefully and ready. I 'came out' as a white ghost with wings and I floated up. I could see my friend by my bedside with my body. I went through white clouds and came to a beautiful place that had so much in it at once: beds of clouds, mountains to the right, waterfall to the left, love and light and sun everywhere. There were white horses in front of a rainbow. Everything looked beautiful: it was amazing.

HEALING OUTCOMES

From a very young age my daughter had a dislike of getting her hands dirty, and of doing chores. I also felt that whatever I did was never enough for her. I found myself picking on things she did for no logical reason, and at times felt the same illogical rage boil up when attempting to communicate with her. I recognised that we were acting out a cycle of events, with the roles reversed. My other daughter was the lynch pin that had kept me company and held me to the present, when in that lifetime all I wanted to do was escape. She supported and helped me on a daily basis, in her role of peace-keeper and translator.

One of my sayings to my daughter when she came to that age where they are very demanding was: "I'm not your servant!" My other daughter, who had been the other servant in that lifetime, also used this term to her sister, independently of me.

This regression helped me to understand what was going on in the communication between me and my daughter, whom I had found difficult to understand. I felt that this regression helped me to understand her more. After I had died, this lady was shown to me: her husband had left her, and in Victorian society this was disgraceful. Through no fault of her own she was now an abandoned woman, but the money and house had been hers, so her husband had left her in it. For some reason he just walked out and went abroad, so although she was financially secure, she was still ostracised by the community. She was bitter and resentful and took it out on my friend and me: her servants. As I understood all this, I felt sorry for her and realised how difficult her life was.

However, I felt that I had missed some learning outcomes and although I made many connections, I wanted to recall what had happened after the lady threw my writing in the fire. I had a feeling that I had attacked her, and possible even killed her. But the way that the regression was structured, meant that I had not the time, or the guiding to go back to that image in the drawing room, in order to explore it further.

This regression was also different as we were told to go back and amend anything we didn't like, as we went through the experience. I found that by doing this, I missed important information that I felt I needed to know. When I did change the bad bits, I had the lady like my stories and congratulate me on them. I had her help me get them published. I had it so that my friend and I lived together on my earnings as a writer, and the lady would visit us for tea on equal terms as a friend.

Anon

ANALYSIS

Denise Linn is a very experienced and spiritual past life guide. Anon's experience was highly detailed and coloured – she recalled with all her senses. She recognised a stallholder in the market but couldn't place him in her current life. This would indicate that she had not yet met him in her current life, and it is possible that she never will.

Often conflicted relationships are replayed over and over throughout several lifetimes until a resolution is reached. Anon felt that her relationship with her eldest daughter was doing just this. From the strength of her emotion towards her mistress, I think that this Victorian life is not the initial lifetime relating to her difficulties with her daughter. It is also likely that, if left, this conflict would continue into future lifetimes. By experiencing this past life Anon has the opportunity to break this cycle now, and heal this conflict. At some point I would recommend that she return to this past life memory at the point at which she was challenged by her mistress in the drawing room.

The fact that she died in bed as a servant indicates that she didn't murder her mistress, but the 'boiling rage' she experienced needs to be more fully explored as this part of the regression was left unexplained due to the way the regression was structured.

STYLE

This regression was part of a past life seminar run by Denise Linn, in London, to which oddly enough, I also attended. Several hundred people were there and we underwent a mass group regression. It was a fascinating experience. Although there were many people there to support us if anyone should have a distressing experience, it was still a deeply personal event.

Unfortunately in group regressions, you have to move at the guides' pace, and in this instance Anon was moved out of the drawing room before the confrontation with her mistress had fully played out.

The idea of changing the outcome is to change the future residue. So if you have brought forward any issues or problems relating to that lifetime, making those changes can help diminish the problems in the current lifetime. It is good way of helping to clear the blocks, but I would recommend that you recall the lifetime as it was in its entirety, right through the death experience, before you rerun it and make changes.

In this chapter I included Anon's experience of approaching the past life and the after death experience of going into Spirit as this was one of the most descriptive images of the spirit world that I have heard. Every experience is different, and the method you use to access past lives will influence that experience. Denise Linn is very big on guiding you through the spirit world, and I too have found this technique to be very beneficial.

CHAPTER SEVEN

'THE PREGNANT NUN'

(Hypnotherapy-training session)

Deborah's experience

*"This lifetime is a chapter in the book
of your existence."*

CH

"I was training in Scotland when we practiced this method – 'The Christos Method'. It was a very different and interesting, but time consuming process. I had no preconceived ideas as I accessed this past life; I just left my mind open to whatever my subconscious wanted to show me. Needless to say it was very enlightening; one of the most profound experiences I have had from a past life regression." Deborah

THE PREGNANT NUN

I found myself in a market place. It is a pretty dull and dismal time. I feel very aware of wearing a long, rough black robe, black boots and a strange, white hat with curled up points. For some reason I thought of Dutch hats. I knew was a nun.

The ground of the marketplace was made up of chunky, oblong, grey 'cobbles'. A huge, ugly, grey building dominated the scene. One of the walls of the building seemed to surround the town, so the town was enclosed. I was shopping in the market, going from stall to stall to select produce, but I felt very strange within this body: I felt very heavy and uncomfortable and was particularly aware that I was naked under my robe. I had a heavy feeling in my stomach and between my legs. I knew I wasn't a virgin, and this disturbed me, as I knew I was a nun. I had a tight, brown leather strap above my belly, which was incredibly uncomfortable and caused me constant distress, but I was not allowed to remove it. Then suddenly I realised that I was heavily pregnant and that my child was due within days. I was about 20 years old. The date was hard to place and could have been anytime between 1400-1700. Wherever I was, it was a very backwards place.

I looked at my hands and saw they were fine and delicate, like a lady's. I certainly hadn't worked with my hands at all. I became aware that I had been put in the convent as a punishment for being a pregnant, unmarried woman. I was from a good family, to whom I was now an embarrassment.

The air around me was clean and cool: although I wasn't dressed for winter and I was cold – perhaps the situation was set high up, in the mountains. I was in Belgium, and the town was called Liege? (Pronounced Leejez.)

Although I wore this huge hat, underneath I was aware that I had short, dark hair that had been hacked off. I felt very depressed, emotionally numb, betrayed and very lonely. The Colditz style surroundings depressed me, and this was a very poor area.

Next I found myself in the dining hall of the convent. It is a large, long, medieval style hall. The room is dark and cold with a fireplace at the other end. Along the length, in the middle, is a long, dark wooden table, with two benches either side. There must have been about 12 nuns in total in the dining hall at that time and we were eating a meal. No one spoke at all: I think it was a silent order.

All the women there were much older than me. They were not nice women: I could feel their animosity towards me, like something tangible in the air. I remember thinking that I was surrounded by people, yet still alone. I was mind numbingly depressed and bored. I had no one to talk to, or to express my feelings to.

For this meal we ate from pewter plates with our fingers, although I felt that we used spoons for a meal if it was appropriate to. We ate green vegetables, (curly kale?) potatoes, and a heavy, stodgy gruel, still with our fingers. The food was tasteless and boring. I hated these women. They were supposed to be God's helpers in the community but they were just a bunch of twisted, jealous, petty, old, vindictive women. I could feel them judging me, their eyes were filled with disgust, and they made my life miserable although they never spoke, at least not to me. I had never heard anyone speak since I had been confined here. I felt that my name was Barbara.

I found myself back in the marketplace with a wooden cart pulled by a mule. I have a small leather drawstring purse that hangs from my excruciatingly uncomfortable strap. The discomfort was permanent. The marketplace was very busy, I realised that everyone there must see that I am both a novice nun and pregnant, but it seemed to be ignored. Actually no one looked at me, approached me or had any contact with me unless I directly spoke to them in relation to making a purchase. It was like I didn't exist. The stalls in the market were made up of wooden timbers covered in material. There was coarse, yellow straw strewn around on the ground, it had rained recently so there was a smell of dirty, wet straw. I am here to buy cloth and vegetables, but I am confused, as I know we grow vegetables in the convent garden.

Suddenly I see a man I know across the market, looking at some goods on a stall. I know him, he is the father of my child and his name is Armand. He is well dressed in a loose white shirt, tan trousers and knee-high boots. He has very short auburn hair, and he is an artist. I have a sudden urge to approach him and speak to him. But instead I watch him for a while: he takes ages inspecting the trinkets at the stall. Suddenly I recognise him as a male friend in my current lifetime. I then change my mind about approaching him: I don't want to talk to him, as he didn't care about me. He had no interest in marrying me and no interest in the child. We were neither of us peasants but from good families, but in a poor region that doesn't mean much. I felt that even if I did want to speak to him, it would be inappropriate for me to approach him. He doesn't see me, and after watching him for a few more minutes I turn away and return to the convent. I realised that I felt nothing for him anymore, and I found it hard to recall how I did feel about him. I didn't feel anything at that time at all.

The entrance to my abode is a huge grey archway with the same shaped wooden doors. The mouth to Hell.

The next significant event was giving birth to my child. I feel it but I was still not allowed to remove the tight strap across the top of my belly, and it caused me incredible discomfort throughout the labour and birth. It is panicking me.

(Suddenly in my mind I flash forwards to this lifetime when I was in labour with my 1st child, and at the hospital they attached a black plastic belt that monitored the baby's heartbeat, and it felt exactly the same as this strap. In this lifetime I wanted them to remove it, and they refused, which almost led to me freaking out.)

I had the child and it was a girl. Two nuns were with me and they immediately took her away. I was confused and I didn't know if I was relieved or not. For a second I thought they were going to throw her out of the window and kill her – I had heard of this before. But they didn't. Maybe because it was a girl? I suddenly felt a painful wrench and had the feeling that I was experiencing how it felt to have a child taken from you. It was obvious that I was not going to be allowed to raise her myself. I thought she would be given to a family, or raised by nuns in another part of the convent. I was certain that I would never see her again.

The day I died I found myself high up on the roof of the convent. It was a very, very high building. I get the impression it was built up a mountain. It had the crenulated edges as on castles. I am looking out at the surrounding countryside. It's very green and it stretches for miles, we must be very isolated. I am considering throwing myself off the building. I become aware of one of the nuns approaching me across the roof from behind. I turn around to see the nun. She is holding my daughter who is now about 18 months or 2 years old. She looks like me: she has curly brown hair and huge round brown eyes. The nun carries her on her hip, and the baby watches me. She knows who I am. I recognise her now, and I think she is my brother in my current lifetime.

Suddenly I am falling backwards over the edge of the roof. I didn't jump. I feel like I have been pushed, but the nun seems too far away. I am too surprised to scream. I lie on the rocks on my back at the base of the building. I look briefly up at the building and the sky before I die. "I wonder what they'll do with my body." I leave that body. I feel pissed off but there's nothing that I can do now. I am relieved to be free, but sad at a wasted young life. It is 1867, 100 years before my current life birth year.

Then I am floating up above my body. I float up to the roof level and I see the nun looking down at my body on the ground far below. But the child can see me – she is watching me as I float up higher and higher. As I look at her I know she will grow up to be someone very important and powerful.

HEALING OUTCOMES

At first I thought this was just a rather grim and woeful tale, and apart from recognising two people in my current lifetime and having the flashback, or flash forward to my 1st child's birth, and the same feelings of panic regarding the monitor, I didn't initially think much more of this past life experience.

However, as very often happens, over the next few days as I processed the information and the implications, a number of connections came to light.

When I was four years old in my current lifetime I went to a convent for my schooling. I absolutely hated it from the first day, and rebelled at every possible opportunity. I hated it to such a degree, that after one particularly bad term, I flatly refused to go back. Unfortunately it was in the last year, but I thought I had made my point! For many years I had nightmares about being trapped in the convent. I could remember every room and passage; every smell, and one of my nightmares was always getting lost and not being able to find my way out. Incidentally the nightmare stopped after this regression.

Porridge used to make me physically ill as a child, and my Mum used to insist we ate it in winter before we went to school.

I still have the 'alone in the crowd' syndrome. But it doesn't bother me – I enjoy my own company in this life. But I do still feel like I don't belong anywhere.

I was given up for adoption in my current lifetime, and it has created issues of rejection. I think that this regression showed me the opposite side of the coin as it were – how it felt to have a child and having it taken away from you. So I have also effectively felt abandonment from the opposite perspective. In my current life I didn't particularly want children, and when I was pregnant I hated it. Although I love my children, my body hated the experience and I was ill for nine months, both times.

Also being rejected by society for being unmarried and pregnant, and being shoved into a convent so you don't embarrass the family was pretty harsh. I did wonder why then, was I sent to get the produce from the market. Upon reflection I think it was deliberate, to humiliate me, as everyone seemed to ignore me like I wasn't there. The moral hypocrisy was evident everywhere – women being scapegoats for men's actions, ie takes two to be in a relationship, but Armand got off scott free and carried on like nothing had happened, and I paid a high price for our relationship. As for the nuns' attitude: so much for Christian charity and forgiveness. I had a natural distrust and dislike of organised religion that I have now resolved. Although I am spiritual I do not believe in the concepts of God, Satan, Heaven or Hell.

I have a thing about standing on the very edge of cliffs, and rooftops, ever since I was very small. It used to scare my parents witless when they took me somewhere with a drop, they'd find me standing right on the edge. I remember always wondering what it would be like to just step off. I think it is the nearest experience we can have to flight, but you obviously die. People always seem to think that killing yourself is 'the easy way out.' It has always annoyed me. It actually takes a lot of courage to decide to end your own life, and then to do it successfully.

Armand, in this life is a very close, platonic male friend, but interestingly his attitude to marriage and children are very similar. He is just not interested. I have never trusted people with auburn hair. I had a friend once with amazing auburn hair – but it took me a long time to accept her as a friend, and I never really trusted her. (No offence intended to those with red hair!)

My child in that lifetime was my younger brother in this lifetime. When he was young he was sometimes really angry and aggressive. As he witnessed my death, in that lifetime and saw me leave my body, he is I think, a pretty advanced soul. By my death, I must have committed that child to a dismal lifetime, if the nuns treated her the same as they did me. This may explain, in part, my brother's anger towards me. Now, he is a happy and contented young man and we get on really well.

Deborah

ANALYSIS

This was a many layered past life, and the connections continue to appear even now, some years after this regression. The convent nightmare has never returned which indicates that something important was resolved upon this regression, and this is often the case where nightmares or repetitive dreams are involved. Connections and relationships with men are highlighted in this regression and also my attitudes towards them. Having a close platonic relationship with my fiend in this lifetime (Armand in that one) has also helped me a great deal. Having to deal with unwanted pregnancy, forced incarceration and social isolation brought up a lot of anti-establishment feelings that I carry in this lifetime too. It has helped me to understand the unfairness of life, but most importantly the fact that you have a choice about whether you let any experience negatively affect you. You can either let it overcome you, or you can grieve for it, accept it, heal it and then move on. I choose the latter.

STYLE

This memory was accessed via the Christos method. It was a very long, slow process, but deeply relaxing. It can be a frustrating process as it requires a long time – this session lasted for 3 hours. Also at least three people are required for this method (see Chapter 13 How to Access Your Past Lives).

I didn't feel any emotional trauma or discomfort apart from *remembering* the physical discomfort of the strap around me all the time. The benefit of this method was that it gave me a long time to get into the regression, and the whole process went at my pace, as it does in a one to one hypnosis session. I found that I didn't accumulate understanding simultaneously – this was needed at the end of the regression. Further information came to me a few days later, which is common in many past life recollections.

CHAPTER EIGHT

'THE CRUSADER'

(Day meditation)

Clare's experience

*"Fear of death
is only fear of the unrecalled"*

NH

"I live in Bristol, where I am a massage therapist, Reiki teacher and workshop leader. My interest in past lives was sparked during a very profound Reiki treatment, when my first incarnation manifested itself in the room. I believe that by accessing the memories & experiences of past incarnations, the karma each of us carries forward one life to the next, can be released. As a consequence we are led towards a more fulfilled existence, towards finding our true life purpose and guided closer to the attainment of enlightenment." Clare Hawtin

THE CRUSADER

I am dressed in chain mail and I am wearing a long, white tabard with a red cross on the front. I am dressed as a Christian knight in the Crusades. I have a sword. I am a woman. I am tall and thin, in my 40's. I am being arrested. I am frightened and full of dread.

My arms are painfully pulled up behind my back by one man, who's saying angrily: "Take her to the king!" The two soldiers each take an arm, holding them behind me, and they march me off. I get the feeling that I have spoken out and my opinions have upset the authorities.

Then I am lying on the rack: a tortuous stretching machine and I am being tortured. I know instinctively that I am here because of my beliefs, because I have spoken my truth and will not relinquish this. I feel my right arm pull out of its socket at the shoulder as I am stretched. I feel tremendous pain through my shoulder and the surrounding muscles. I feel calm and accept my fate.

Then I see myself lying down being drawn and quartered. I come out of the experience before I die in that lifetime. I ask, 'is this me?' The answer is yes. The person I am in this particular incarnation looks like one of my spiritual guides (she symbolises courage). I ask, 'are you my guide?' The answer is yes.

As these answers come, a huge release of energy comes from my shoulder, and the pain I have been experiencing dissipates.

HEALING OUTCOMES

I have always thought that perhaps my spiritual guides (or at least some of them) are my past incarnations. This particular guide has always represented courage.

I have had a problem with my shoulder for some time, since I experienced police brutality during a march. At that time, two policemen pulled my arms back behind my back. My arms were manipulated much further than they should have been, so I endured a physical injury, and have also carried an emotional trauma because of this event. The police brutality aroused such a strong emotional response that it has affected me. It mirrored that past life experience, and I understand how that past life had such a dramatic effect on my current life.

Speaking my truth has always been a challenge for me throughout my current life, and I have done a lot of work on this over the past few years. Since my past life experience I have had little shoulder pain and I have healed the emotional trauma associated with it. Both the injury sustained in this life, and the karma of the past life seem to have been lifted. I am also more confident, more centred, more able to speak my truth, and my healing work (I am a Reiki practitioner) has reached a deeper level, which is expansive and hugely powerful. I feel free.

Past life recall has confirmed my belief that I have lived before. It confirms how we carry memory from past lives in current life mind and body.

Clare Hawtin

ANALYSIS

This is a wonderful example of a past life experience repeating itself in the present life. Clare's experience at the march mirrored a past life trauma, and this triggered her past life memory, allowing her arrest trauma and her past life experience to be released. Subsequently, Clare's shoulder injury could now heal itself, as the cellular memory of the past life had also been relieved.

Often an injury in a past life reoccurs in the present as a reminder that there is some unresolved healing from the past to be
undertaken. Events conspire to produce a situation whereby this
replay can happen in the current lifetime.

Meditation is a spiritual state of mind from which past life regression and astral travel are possible.

Clare recognised that some of her spirit guides seem to be past
incarnations. This one represented courage. In his book 'Life Between Lives' Michael Newton explains that we leave part of ourselves in Spirit, to continue learning. Clare's experience would indicate that some guides are aspects of our soul, known also as our
Higher Self.

STYLE

Clare experienced this spontaneous past life recall during a meditation. She was taking part in a ten-day 'vipassanna', which teaches
one to observe sensations, cravings, and aversions and to become
equanaminous as a way to remove misery from our beings, including misery that has been brought through from previous lives.

CHAPTER NINE

'AFRICAN HEALER'

(Self-hypnosis)

Anon's experience

*"It is not the life we have that is important
but how we live it"*

CH

"I had hypnosis for weight loss several years ago and as part of that process I was taught self-hypnosis which I have used ever since for minor pain relief, relaxation and the like. I thought I would try and access a past life using this method and focussing on some nature music, as I wanted help with my creative writing. I was feeling a bit daunted by the 'hugeness' of everything at that time. I was very surprised by the information and healing I received, and it has helped me immensely." Anon

AFRICAN HEALER

I am in Africa, a beautiful place. I am walking along a dusty track. I am extremely tall, slender and dark brown. I have very short dark hair and I am wearing a colourful patterned shift-dress and have nothing on my feet. I have hoops in my ears. I think I have a head-piece, but if so it feels close to my hair. I am 32 years old.

I am approaching a village of grass huts. Slightly apart from the others is a single grey round straw hut. A man comes out to greet me. He smiles and welcomes me into his house. He is about ten years older than I am. As I passed into the man's house I silently asked "Do I know you?" and I recognised him as John, a man I worked with in this lifetime. He had the same smile and manner.

I was treated as if I was a visiting dignitary. I felt that I was important, yet I had the greatest respect for him and saw him as a wise man: an equal. I carried myself erect and I felt very self contained, dignified, knowledgeable, and calm and content. I felt confident and competent.

(I was confused at how tall I felt, it seemed unnaturally tall!)

I entered his house and sat on the rush floor facing the stone circle. The hut was bare. I looked up at the roof and saw the sunlight through the hole in the top. We sat and talked, in an African dialect and then we got up and went to the entrance. He pointed the way for me to go. He was a 'greeter'. His role was to meet travellers, assess them, and then to show them where to go. It was a welcoming ritual. He had the authority to turn people away.

I then found myself walking into the village: five or six huts were to my left, close together. I saw a couple of women outside and became aware that only the women were here at the moment.

It was a very peaceful community. I administered healing to an elderly lady and also to a couple of children. I saw myself holding a small child's wrist and rubbing something into his palm. I knew I was a healer and a wise woman. My skills must have been different or sought after, as I travelled from village to village in a nomadic manner. I was talking to some women, offering advice. I was not always giving herbal healing. I had no particular tools or equipment with me as such, just a little bag. I knew these people, so I obviously came here regularly.

In the regression, I wanted to see the place that I lived and into my head flashed an image of a large hut with shelves holding wooden bowls. The hut smelt of herbs and concoctions. It was not near here.

I went forward to the end of that life. I was lying on a plain wooden bed-like structure. I was uncovered and lying on my back. I was about 45, or 48 years old. I was dying and I had a flutter of pain in my lower stomach area. There were several people around me, perhaps six. An elderly man was by my head to my left, and a younger woman by my head to my right. I knew the man, and again I silently asked "Who are you?" but I do not know him yet in this lifetime. The girl on my right leaned down towards me and smiled, I recognised her as my eldest daughter in this lifetime. Then I died and drifted off. I found myself floating around the sun twice, before I went away.

HEALING OUTCOMES

I entered this regression with the specific intention of linking with past skills and knowledge. I was hoping to bring back something that would help me as a writer, struggling with the many burdens that that lifestyle brings, to help me get in touch with my intuitive writing nature.

I was somewhat surprised to appear as an African healer, as I have no particular affinity with Africa. Regarding healing I have always believed in the herbal, natural approach, so this fits well with my ethos.

I was surprised at how tall and willowy I felt in the regression and until recently I thought this was my imagination. However, a couple of years ago I came across some statues of African women from the Maasai tribe, all of whom were portrayed exactly as I recalled myself in the past life regression!

I was astounded.

The most striking thing about this regression was the feeling of utter contentment and confidence that accompanied that lifetime. The powerful feeling also of absolute knowledge: I had no inse-curities, no concerns. It was wonderful. I loved the idea that I was a nomadic healer who visited the villages to dispense healing and wisdom. What a simple, wonderful life.

Anon

ANALYSIS

This lifetime reaffirmed for Anon that the simple life was the easi-est and most natural state of being. All her needs were met: food, satisfying job, friends, and roof over her head. Perhaps this was an important message for Anon's aspired life as a writer – keep it simple?

She also felt that she did not speak a lot during this lifetime. Silence seemed to be highly valued; Anon did not 'chat' to the people she came across, but shared wisdom. 'Speak not unless it is of value' sprung to her mind. Anon felt that all she needed to say in this life was possible with a smile, a gentle touch and a few words if necessary. Perhaps this is all you really need?

Anon felt grateful for this lifetime, as she had never experi-enced a feeling of being so complete, so sure and so comfortable with what she was doing. Another message perhaps that writing was right and most natural for her in this lifetime, as it had been the reason she sought this regression?

Anon also recognised the man who was with her when she died, but knew she had not met him yet.

In this hectic age it is a wonderful experience to regress to a life-time that was simple and where you were content. Contentment is often missing from this modern world, as is a sense of belonging to something much bigger. This past life acted as a reminder to Anon that the simplest lifestyle is the most natural state of existence.

STYLE

Self-hypnosis is a very useful tool for past life regression. You will need to learn the technique, preferably from a hypnotherapist, and this can be done in one short session. Like any technique, you will need to practise it until you feel confident to regress yourself. You will then be able to take yourself into the hypnotic state and visu-alise a creative journey leading you into a past life.

CHAPTER TEN

'WIDOWER'S GUILT'

*(Audiotape guided regression
by Denise Linn: 'Past Lives & Beyond')*

Lynda's experience

"Life is a dance – make sure you join in"

CH

"After being on a spiritual and personal growth path for a few years, I discovered past life regression through my friend Deborah (the author). The following story came out of my query regarding failed relationships, including my marriage that ended in divorce. I felt at the right stage to delve deeper into my psyche to reveal the area that needed healing." Lynda

WIDOWER'S GUILT

I find myself standing on a large rock looking down a sheer cliff with treetops a long way down!

I am very hot as the sun is beating down upon my head: it is a beautiful day.

I become aware that I am a Native American male, wearing nothing but a skin loincloth. I am muscular and fit: I am in my 30's. I have stripped myself of all my personal belongings and decorations, in preparation for what I must do.

I am feeling intensely distraught, and I am about to jump to my death.

Looking at where this feeling comes from, I discover that my wife and two young children have been murdered. I think it's possible that they were murdered as a personal attack on my family, not on the village, or tribe. I feel it could be connected to my wife's status, as she was the daughter of the Tribe Chief.

I feel an incredible sense of guilt that I could have been there but wasn't. I should have been there. Maybe I was away doing something else, something trivial. I feel that I was able to prevent their deaths, but for some reason that I have not gone into, I was not there and have therefore dishonoured my wife's family, the whole tribe and myself. My only course of action is to take my own life to restore the honour of our families and that of the tribe.

There the regression ends, knowing that my task was complete.

I didn't re-experience the death scene itself, but I could 'see' myself jumping off and knew what it would feel like to do it. I had an understanding of the death experience.

HEALING OUTCOMES

This regression has shown me how I have brought feelings of guilt forward in time. From as far back as I can remember, where relationships have been concerned, I have always given everything of myself to my partners in particular, and friends and family to a degree.

I felt I had to be 'on call' for everyone's needs – I had to be there for them: to carry things, especially their emotional baggage; to try to fix their lives and make everything better for them. It satisfied me to help everyone and anyone.

Basically I wore a HEAVY rucksack and became a doormat.

To my relief the turning point came after this past life regression. I now no longer magnetise needy people, which shows me that the reflection of my own neediness is dissolving, and I had been taking away other peoples power to heal and live their own lives. I feel light and free to pursue my future, having sent love, understanding and compassion to that guilt-ridden part of me that needed healing. Over the last few years my strength and inner resolve has increased to help me through the challenges and to enjoy the good bits of being a single parent of two wonderful teenage daughters. I pray with gratitude for the opportunity to heal and share my experiences.

Lynda from Somerset

ANALYSIS

In this regression the feeling of guilt and the need to put it right were the dominant factors. To give his own life to right the wrongs done to his family and tribe was not only expected, but a heavy price to pay. This 'self-sacrifice' resulted in Lynda's current need to 'sacrifice' herself in her relationships.

Focussing on the emotion of being 'intensely distraught' accessed the significance of this past life. It was then that the reasons for the intended suicide became clear. Focussing on pain or emotion in this way often creates a shortcut, or direct route to understanding the issues to be resolved.

Lynda didn't physically re-experience the death experience of this past life but saw it and spiritually encompassed the relevant meaning. It isn't always necessary to *physically* re-experience the death scene to access healing. Sometimes the death itself is not the direct cause of the current trauma. In this regression, the reason for the act of self-sacrifice; that guilt, had created issues for Lynda. Generally speaking, if you need to *physically* experience the trauma of the death for healing purposes, then you will; if you don't, you won't.

Lynda has always had a very strong sense of family with the Native American Indians. As a child she played 'Cowboys and Indians', when she supported the Indians and this sense of belonging and support followed through into the films she watched, where she was always on the side of the American Indians.

Needy people have been attracted to Lynda, as she has a caring and loving nature, which enables the needy to grow, feeling supported. As she acknowledges, this reflected a need to be needed within herself. She has rediscovered her inner strength and as she has done so, has found that she no longer attracts such needy types. Now if needy people are within her circle, Lynda has the strength to help them help themselves, without getting sucked in to a give-away situation.

STYLE

Audiotapes and CDs are inexpensive and serve a useful, if brief introduction to past life regression through relaxation and self-hypnosis. This past life was recalled using a guided audiotape regression by Denise Linn.

The drawback of this method is that the session, including the guided relaxation introduction only lasts 30 minutes. Although the regression got straight to the point, it allows little time to fully explore the lifetime, nor the opportunity to go back and change any negative outcomes.

However, this is a good way to get a sense of a particular lifetime that you may want to further explore in detail by other means.

CHAPTER ELEVEN

'ORKNEY LOVE MATCH'

(One to one therapist regression)

Alison's experience

"Letting go is only for this lifetime"

Alison

"I'd never questioned my life or my belief system. I wasn't in the least bit religious although I did believe in a higher 'something', but I had never had any reason to question that 'something' or look particularly closely at it. Now I found myself asking many questions; I needed to know why." Alison

'ORKNEY LOVE MATCH'

The first thing I focused on was my feet. I was wearing sandals; the leather was rough and their purpose served to be practical as opposed to comfortable. I was wearing a brown tunic that came to mid-thigh: it was made of coarse wool and felt itchy against my skin. The landscape was flat and windy with a distinct lack of trees. The next thing that struck me was a familiar burning smell; the almost sweet smell of burning dung.

(During this lifetime, I have experienced the same smell from the campfires of Kenyan villages.)

I had regressed to a life in a Viking settlement. My name was Marianne Johannson and I was fourteen years old. I was looking after my two young brothers because my parents were both working in the fields. I didn't know the proper name of the village; I only knew it as home. Other people visited our village from other settlements, to trade and arrange marriages.

There was a boy I liked called Jack, who lived in the same village as me but was slightly older and had many admirers. I felt that Jack liked me too.

I moved forward two years. I was standing in the centre of a circle with Jack and people were holding hands and dancing around us; Jack and I were getting married. The lasting memory I have of the experience was the complete happiness and love that I felt at that time.

I then moved forward to the day that I died. I was 29 and died in childbirth, delivering my third child. The most difficult part of that whole experience was letting go. Leaving Jack behind broke my heart yet I knew I had to leave.

HEALING OUTCOMES

1998 was a horrible year for me. Within the space of four weeks between April and May of that year, my twenty eight year old brother died of leukaemia and I buried my fourteen-week-old daughter. Shortly after my daughter died, my marriage had broken down. Grief can bring people closer together or it can polarise them. Our experience had done the latter. I quickly become involved in another relationship that turned out to be extremely emotionally abusive. Looking back on it now, I had used that relationship to punish myself; to live in a perpetual state of grief, devoid of any other emotion. To the outside world, I seemed fine but on the inside I was slowly dying.

Hindsight is a wonderful thing. It was whilst in this relationship in 2003 that I decided to have a past life regression. From the time I booked the regression I felt a strange kind of excitement, which struck me as odd at the time as I hadn't actually experienced any kind of positive feelings for around five years. The significance of those feelings was to become apparent over the next few months.

From the therapist's point of view the most striking part of the regression was my voice, which changed from my usual one to that of a young teenager, and then matured into an adult voice as I went through the regression.

After the regression the therapist joked that if I ever met Jack in this lifetime then there would be fireworks. I did meet 'Jack' and it happened on the Friday the 7th November. Driving to meet him the first time there were firework displays as far as the eye could see. As soon as I met him, I recognised him. The strange thing is he felt the same way although he had never been through the regression and I had never discussed it with him.

There were further coincidences: although he had been previously married, he had always felt as though a part of him was missing in this life; his favourite song for years had been 'Marianne' by a little known group called 'Sisters of Mercy'; he had always felt his spiritual home to be on Orkney (an island off the coast of Scotland), a place that I hadn't visited until last summer. Upon my visit the first thing that struck me was the lack of trees, quickly followed by how windy it is on the island: both of which were evident in my regression. I have no doubt that the Viking settlement was in Orkney as for the whole time I was there, I felt at one with the environment as though it were somewhere I knew well.

'Jack' and I married six months ago and are both very happy together. We both share the feeling that we have found 'home'.

From a healing perspective, it made me realise that whilst letting go in this life is one of the hardest things we can do, the letting go is only for this lifetime. Loved ones may have departed from this life but they will be there again in future ones and until that time, it's a case of living the one we're in through all of its ups and downs.

The weirdest thing of all is just how 'Jack' and I did meet in this lifetime – it was playing Scrabble over the internet! Some things just have to be put down to karma.

Alison

ANALYSIS

In this regression Marianne was devastated at having to leave Jack, after dying in childbirth. In this life she recognised him immediately and they have been brought together to complete unfinished business from that past life.

Alison recognised Orkney as the site of the Viking village as soon as she visited the island. Sometimes there is a 'knowing' that occurs, similar to deja vu, when you visit a place that you lived in during a previous lifetime.

STYLE

This past life regression was accessed using a guided process by a hypnotherapist, with experience in past life regression, on a one to one basis. Hypnosis is one of best methods to access past lives and allows plenty of time to fully explore the lifetime. The therapist should be able to guide you through the death experience and help you analyse the issues affecting you now. Depending on the personal ethos of the therapist, they may not encompass the spirit world, or spend long on the healing aspects. It's important to ask beforehand.

Alison says: "The therapist asked me the name of the village but that confused me, as I only knew the village as home. He asked whether people came to visit from other settlements. I answered that they did. He asked if I was to be married. I was surprised by his question and told him no. He asked if anyone had caught my eye and I told him about Jack. He asked if Jack liked me too and I told him that he did."

Some therapists focus on only a few aspects of the regression experience such as relationships and whom you know now, and may ask somewhat leading questions. In the above example, the best way to phrase some of these questions would have been: "Is your village isolated or is there interaction with other communities?" This is an open question offering more than one answer. "Are you married or are you single?" and "Is there anyone in this lifetime that is special to you in any way?" are all open questions, not leading ones. Some therapists unconsciously project the aspects they are interested in, into the client's experience. As a therapist it can sometimes be difficult to maintain a balance during the questioning process and it's therefore vital to allow the client's answers to lead the questions.

It also has to be remembered that, especially in primitive or isolated communities, facts such as the name of the place, the year, or who is ruling are often irrelevant, particularly when the client has regressed to a child or young adult. Sometimes the overwhelming emotional and physical experiences of that lifetime render the recollection of facts unimportant to the past life explorer; it just doesn't matter to them. This lack of factual information can be disappointing to the therapist, but rarely is of importance or value to the client. The point of the regression is usually to access healing.

CHAPTER TWELVE

'VIOLATIONS OF TRUST'

(Group regression with Roger Woolger)

Catherine's experience

*"Past lives collect in layers like fallen autumn leaves,
we have to rake through them to clear the unconscious."*

DM

"In 1999 I discovered a hard lump in my stomach area. Fibroid tumours were diagnosed. Because of the size and number of the tumours there was talk of surgery to remove my womb. I was 35 and didn't have children. Two healers had independently told me they felt there was a past life connection. I started to get the most horrendous flashback images during meditation. I wouldn't have gone delving into past lives for the sake of it, but the flashback experiences I was having were so disturbing that they demanded attention." Catherine

VIOLATIONS OF TRUST

*(This regression contains graphic references
that some readers may find powerful or unsettling.)*

PART 1

(I was just starting a new relationship and the prospect of becoming sexually active after a period of being single triggered some very deep sexual trauma. I was already 'cooking' before I even got to the workshop. I had recently realised why I had always had such an aversion to the popular plant called 'red hot poker'. This plant is very tall and thin and stands upright with a red tip, looking very much like its name. During meditation I had seen in my mind's eye what had been done to me with a red-hot poker: it had been inserted up inside me.)

There's a circle of people standing around watching and I'm on some sort of bench or table in the middle. It's quite dark. Then it all happened very quickly. At the point at which I re-experienced the searing pain of the red-hot poker being inserted I let out a blood-curdling scream. With all the force I could muster I screamed "No", in a long cry, repeatedly.

(At one point I jumped into another past life where I found myself in a similar setting lying on a table surrounded by a circle of watching people. This time I was younger, just a girl. Again I was being touched in the genital area: the people were taking it in turns. I couldn't tell whether it was a medical procedure

or something more sinister. It certainly didn't feel good, which suggested some sort of ritualised sexual abuse. Roger brought me back to the original scene.)

I ended up with my body very tightly curled up in a foetal position and held that position for quite some time. It was a stance of protection. I held that position until after I had died and moved into the afterlife. It was only then that I was able, very gradually, to start to relax. My legs were numb and limp, and it took a long time for them to come back to life.

Roger suggested I call in a power animal to help. I chose a polar bear, which for me embodies strength and protection.

In order to help my legs recover we asked them what they wanted to do. They chose to run. So as I lay on my side, Roger held a big cushion under my feet to simulate the ground, and I ran as fast as I could away from the scene until I was so exhausted I could run no more. After the session my legs felt quite strange. It felt almost like learning to walk again. I felt quite vulnerable for some time afterwards and was very careful to look after myself well.

PART 2

(During that workshop I spent a lot of the time in a disassociated state because my trauma was being triggered. I was very relieved to have an opportunity to do another related regression. I needed to work on what was simply another layer of the same sexual trauma: rape by a soldier. I knew that the soldier had thrown me down on some stone steps. To help take me into the scene, I asked for something that would simulate those hard stone steps. We found an A4 binder that was perfect for the job. I put this underneath my back and kept it there for the entire regression. It felt very hard and uncomfortable, just as the steps had done.)

I'm a young Catholic nun, about seventeen, wearing a black habit. I see myself in a chapel praying to a statue of the Virgin Mary that the war might end. Then there's chaos and confusion, shouting and screaming. I'm trying to run away from a soldier – he grabs me by the wrist. I get thrown down against the stone steps.

The soldier lifts my black habit up. I become aware of how clenched my buttocks are. I know it's not his fault; that he's not to blame for what he's doing. In desperation I scream "Oh, God, why have you abandoned me?" My fists want to hit him but my heart doesn't want to hurt him. There's a terrible conflict in my fists as I hold them clenched and they shake with the tension. Eventually, after a long time, I start to feel energy, heat and tingling flowing down my arms and into my hands. Slowly, I let go; I surrender. My heart wins over my fists and they fall to my side.

My legs have the same conflict. They try to protect me; they're just doing their job. But I know that struggling and fighting makes it worse, that I just need to surrender. How can I surrender to what this man is doing to me? I hold my legs very tightly wrapped right around each other for a long time before I'm ready to let go. I know that letting go means feeling. I don't want to let go; I don't want to feel what is happening. I don't want to see what is happening. My head is twisted right round to the right. I'm telling myself "this isn't happening, this isn't real."

As Roger talks me through it I resist the memory of the actual rape for some time. I try to talk to my pelvis, to persuade it to feel, to let go. It doesn't want to feel anything. It's shut down. I try to bring it back to life by flexing the pelvic floor muscles. At last I remember that I know what the cold metallic barrel of the rifle feels like inside, so I use that memory to help reawaken the area.

Then I manage to feel the penis. It feels warm and pleasant in comparison with the cold metal. That's the really difficult bit: my heart is terrified but my genitals enjoy it. I don't understand what happens next as the soldier suddenly stops. I'm terrified. The innocent nun doesn't understand why he stops but I, as Catherine know what has happened. Next he smashes my pelvis with the butt of the rifle, shoves the barrel up inside me and pulls the trigger.

Roger claps his hands loudly to mimic the gunshot.

I roll right over but I don't die instantly.

*Roger takes me to the last heartbeat and counts to three. It's
over.*

I start to laugh as I see myself floating around in my nun's habit.
It looks hilarious. I see the other nuns gathering my body up. Now
it's time to move towards the light. At first I'm not ready. Then I
discover to my amazement that I want to take the soldier with me,
towards the light. I have no sense of judgement about what he has
done, only compassion for him.

HEALING OUTCOMES

In 1999 when I discovered the fibroid tumours, my overriding feeling was "I don't want this to be happening to me." Followed in
despair was the question "why is this happening to me?" Eventually, after trying various complementary therapies, I had to have
the hysterectomy. As I coped with my grief I still had no full understanding of why my body had developed the fibroids or what
it was I needed to learn. The sacral area was involved, so I knew
that the issues related to my sexuality. I also knew that it was to do
with male abuse as the tumours had started to form when the relationship I was in turned abusive. Some time later, and seemingly
unrelated, I started to get the most horrendous flashback images
during meditation. I had a strong sense that this was past life material and it was coming up spontaneously. I also found that having
bodywork, in particular massage, was triggering memories held in
my body. Over a period of months the little snippets of memories,
like pieces of a jigsaw puzzle, started to slot together and form
two distinct pictures in my mind's eye. One memory was of being
raped as a female servant in a stable block, by one of the masters
of the house. The other was of the most horrific sexual violation
by the soldier.

I sought out someone who could help me and came across Roger Woolger, an international authority on past life regression. The
timing was perfect for me, as events in my life had conspired to

bring the material right up to the surface. I knew that the memories had to be totally re-experienced in order for the trauma held in my body to be released. I already had a pretty good idea of what I was going to have to deal with. There was a strong part of me that didn't want to do the regression, but the desire to resolve the material was stronger than the fear of having to go through it. I was hoping to be able to minimise the impact of past sexual trauma on my new relationship. I also no longer wanted to be haunted by the flashbacks.

I learnt a phenomenal amount from the regression work. I also healed a great deal. The main areas of learning and healing for me relate to spirituality and to the body.

In terms of my body I learnt that it has a 'mind' of its own, that one part can be in conflict with another. My work now includes learning to be kinder to my body, to show it more respect and to listen to what different parts of it are trying to tell me. The main healing regarding my body is that the regression helped me to come to a place of feeling more accepting of the hysterectomy. It made the pain of the grief a bit more bearable. It became obvious to me as a result of the regression, that the wounds to my feminine sexuality went very deep. Often women who have been raped or sexually violated simply shut down energetically from the waist down. The pelvis says; "I don't want to feel this. I'm not going to feel this." And the body has a phenomenal capacity to protect itself in that way.

The work to get the energy flowing through my legs and to release the immobilised pelvic area continues. I feel very grateful to know what it is that I need to work with. The understanding I gained through the regression about all of this is vital to me.

One of the areas I have really struggled with on my spiritual journey is to remain grounded enough to be able to contain the energy, or the light, when it comes through. The trauma held in my body and being shut down energetically from the waist down, has made it very difficult for me to be grounded, to connect with the earth energy. When I was twenty I ended up in a psychiatric hospital because, as I started to open up spiritually, I simply didn't have a strong enough connection with my body.

In terms of my spirituality and values in this lifetime I came to understand several things. The experience of feeling totally abandoned by God during the regression was harrowing. As a result of that I discovered why it has been so difficult for me to feel any connection in this life with the patriarchal, masculine God presented by Christianity. Alongside that I have been able to explore a deep fear and mistrust of men that I had not previously been conscious of. I also made the connection between feeling abandoned and rejected by my father in this lifetime and by the universal, archetypal 'father' in that life. It has helped me to explore my ongoing search for 'the father'.

I also came to understand from the feelings I felt when praying in the chapel, the deep devotion I feel towards the figure of Mary. For me she embodies love and compassion. This was something very beautiful that came out of the regression work. In terms of my desire not to hurt my aggressor, it seems extraordinary that my priority, rather than try to protect myself, was not to inflict injury on another. I see that as an example of the Buddhist values which I hold very dear in this life, of not harming sentient beings and of non-violence. As I struggle to live these values on a daily basis I can now draw on the qualities of that young nun.

So healing my sexual wounding from these past lives is more than just about having healthy, happy sexual relationships. For me it's also the passport to being able to continue exploring my spirituality safely without the danger of mental health complications. I can go on intensive meditation retreats with so much more confidence now. I still have to work very hard sometimes at getting and staying grounded, but at least I know what I'm working with.

I feel enormous gratitude for this work and for those who have done so much to develop it and make it available, especially Roger Woolger.

Catherine Lucas

ANALYSIS

This is powerful example of physical healing and Catherine has been very courageous in telling

Catherine had a lot of pre-past life regression clues that her physical symptoms were related to a much deeper psychological issue. Spontaneous images came to her through meditation and bodywork also alerted her to a past life physical trauma. Independently, two healers also picked up on a past life connection.

With Roger Woolger's methodology, Catherine's experience is a clear example of how her body needed to physically re-experience that trauma.

Rape and sexual abuse are common themes in past life regression, especially during times of war and internal conflict. In previous eras when war was more hand-to-hand combat, bloody, barbaric and frequent, men were often forced into service and kept away from their home and families for many years. The lifestyle was harsh and full of horror. Many of the men were religious and had been brought up to believe that killing was wrong: an act against God, only to find that their government demanded that they commit atrocities. It was extremely difficult for them to reconcile these conflicting values. For many men, the only way they could relieve the stress and trauma of their experience was to rampage and rape whenever they got the chance. This attitude was common of both invading and homeland forces, who caused destruction as they travelled through the country. Some men succumbed to the constant brutality and allowed it to override their individual personality (see 'Viking Hatred').

The act of raping a woman is one of violence: it is a way for an emotionally impotent man to exert his will and regain feelings of power. In this instance the soldier would feel that he has temporarily gained some control over his life. Nuns were virginal brides of

God, and therefore the rape of a nun symbolised a double violation: by his action, the soldier was sticking two fingers up to the
God who had both created and destroyed his life.

From the Nun's point of view we see the conflict that arises
from the belief that God will protect her from her enemies, and the
harsh reality of the real world. This creates a degree of shock and
betrayal both by God, to whom she had devoted her life, and by
the belief she has that it is wrong to harm another. Frequently this
conflict results in the client being anti-religious in the current life.

In this regression, the desire for the nun not to hurt her attacker
emanates from a deeply spiritual belief that killing is wrong. In
Catherine's experience she felt an overwhelming urge to take the
soldier with her into Spirit. During the attack and after her death
she could feel the soldier's fear, horror and pain, and forgave him.
The conflict of experiencing forced sex, but the discovery that her
body enjoyed the sensation is one that arises frequently in such
cases. The emotional distress this paradox creates is often one of
the hardest to resolve. The body is designed to enjoy sex, but the
unorthodox circumstance of the rape situation creates emotional
conflict. Taking a 'bigger picture' view during healing can help to
alleviate this trauma.

A traumatic or brutal rape in a past life can have a similar effect
as an attack on the current life. For example a young woman could
recognise a deep distrust of all men, in her current lifetime, but
not consciously know why. The feelings experienced by a person
who has been raped in a past life often mirror those of someone
having been raped in their current life: feelings of shock, violation,
guilt and horror of the event can lead to problems regarding sexual
confidence, lack of trust in men and issues of self-loathing and loss
of self-esteem. Putting these past life experiences into perspective
by using the 'world view', which includes considering the setting,
era, world motives, spiritual lessons, and the perpetrators pain and
suffering, can heal the conflicts and overcome all these issues.

There have been numerous cases whereby past life regression
and bodywork meditation have healed physical problems where

surgery had been previously recommended. The American author Brandon Bays experienced this phenomenon and recounts her story in her book 'The Journey.' Using past life regression as a tool to understanding the signals your body is sending you can be a powerful way of accessing physical healing.

However, experiencing traumatic situations and life changing events is also part of the learning process on our path to spiritual enlightenment. We chose our bodies and our life experiences, specifically to learn certain lessons that we need. Some of these lessons are very hard, but our higher wisdom understands that we need these experiences and traumas in order to grow.

STYLE

Roger Woolger, like Denise Linn is a renowned regression therapist. His methods are very different to other therapists and he includes art and a certain amount of 'props'. I too, have experienced Roger's methods of regression and found them very enlightening. Workshops are usually a good introduction to past life regression and are supported by trained and experienced therapists.

CHAPTER THIRTEEN

HOW TO ACCESS YOUR PAST LIVES

WHAT CAN I EXPECT?

The experience differs from person to person, and also upon the technique and the individual guiding the experience. Generally a past life regression is a physically deeply relaxing experience, but emotionally and mentally tiring! This sounds like a paradox, but your mind is being very active: accessing and processing long forgotten memories. It is not unusual to feel tired and drained after a regression. Drinking a glass of water and having something light to eat can help you ground yourself in the here and now. It is also useful to write down what you experienced while it is fresh in your mind. Regardless of the method used, you will usually remember everything but keeping a note of your experiences and how you felt about them allows you greater recall at a later date.

With hypnosis, which can be used with about 95% of people who attempt it, the experience can be highly coloured, including sound effects and smells, much like experiencing a movie. Some of my clients however, have had feelings and emotions that they could link to certain events, although they couldn't see any visual information at all. Despite this the emotions and feelings were so strong that we were able to work on healing these sensations.

Most people experience physical sensations, like heat, pain and discomfort, or at the other end of the spectrum: pleasure, comfort, contentment, and happiness. Often the sense of smell is heightened where the visual images are lacking.

In one instance my client, John, could hear talking and laughing even as he approached his past life. He could even smell meat cooking and he got a distinct sense of camaraderie, hustle and bustle of a busy market town. He was clearly experiencing a past life although he couldn't see anything. Intuitively I suspected a cause, but being aware that I couldn't put ideas into John's head I asked him if he knew what a potato was. "Of course I do!" came the brusque response. I asked him to describe it to me. "It's round and hard, smooth and smells a bit sour sometimes." This answer confirmed my suspicions: John had described how the potato felt and smelt, not how it looked: he was blind. Yet despite this he could still pick up an incredible sense of the events, and had a successful regression.

I and many other people have had a combination of these experiences. I have found in my studies that the past lives that have the most negative effects on the current life are those that can be recalled in full and glorious colour, but it is not conclusive: very much depends on your ability to visualise, and this is something that can improve with practise and experience. If you don't consider yourself to be particularly visual, then don't worry: it is very rare indeed not to get something out of a regression experience.

One of the most valuable lessons I learnt was to expect the unexpected. Like John, who could only smell and hear the sounds in the medieval marketplace, Marcus too, when he initially entered the past life could only see darkness. This can sometimes indicate that the explorer has died, before he goes into the light of the spirit world, or that he has not managed to access a past life. Marcus found himself in this situation, but could mover neither forward nor backwards. After some questioning I discovered that Marcus was still in Sprit, but refused to go into his next life. He didn't like living on the Earth plane, and was reluctant to incarnate into his current life. We spent the entire session in Spirit, working on healing the difficulties he had with living on the Earth. He knew he had to incarnate in order to learn more about communicating with other people, and to form relationships. Eventually he was able to move forward and entered the memory of the womb for this lifetime.

During one of my training courses, the Christos method was demonstrated to us on a volunteer student and one of the tutors asked him where he was. "London," he answered. The tutor tried to get the explorer to elaborate without success, so he asked the explorer to look around him. "Do you know what street you are in? Look at a road sign and tell me what it says." The explorer couldn't. There is not much point asking a 10 year old Victorian barrow boy to read a street sign: most working class children couldn't read or write. These things have to be taken into consideration when guiding a regression, so use creative questioning but don't give the explorer scenarios or leading questions. With experience it is surprising how creative you can be when exacting information from a past life explorer!

Mary experienced a lifetime with me where she couldn't move around the building she was in. When I asked her where she was she said, "I am sitting in my armchair knitting." But she couldn't move out of it. It transpired that she was disabled but her daughter had cruelly put her in an armchair for the day, instead of putting her in her wheelchair where she could be mobile.

RECOGNISING PEOPLE

In your past lives there will be people that you know from the current lifetime. Some people will instantly be able to recognise their friends and family as characters in their past lives, as I did in the 'Pregnant Nun.' Sometimes it is not so easy – they will look different, and may even be a different sex, but there is a certain something about that person that usually allows you to recognise them in a past life. Perhaps it is their soul characteristics: there is just a 'knowing.' Often the identifying feature is in the eyes, or the expression in the eyes. The saying 'eyes are the windows of the soul', is no myth.

I have experienced several past lives where I know someone really well and recognise him or her on a soul level, but also know that I have not yet met him or her in my current lifetime. Once I dreamt about a past life lover, and two weeks later recognised him as a stranger, walking down a crowded street. It is a very strange feeling, but is not particularly unusual. You may never meet that person in this lifetime, or you may yet have to meet them, but either way, this is a fascinating aspect of the process.

You will not always meet people you know now, in your past life but don't worry. Remember that when you access a past life, it is like looking in through someone's window – you are observing a small part of that lifetime. You may well have been with your parents, your partner or your children, but that part of the past life you needed to see, may not include them.

Remember also, that the people you know in this lifetime you know in varying degrees of familiarity. The same goes for past lives: for example you may be close to your son in this lifetime, but in that past life, you may only just have met so he would not feature as particularly significant in that lifetime. Likewise your foreign cousin could have been your husband in a past life. You may not know him very well, but meeting him again in this lifetime is a reminder of that intense relationship. You may have chosen to come together to continue that relationship or to experience another kind of friendship.

If you meet someone in a past life and he or she seems familiar, ask if you know them now. You will usually get a response and the answer may well surprise you.

THE DEATH SCENE

The death scene should be experienced in order to get a full idea of any problems that that lifetime has caused you. Often it is the decisions and promises made either on the deathbed, or whilst dying, that have serious negative influences in this life. It is not always necessary to *physically* re-experience a traumatic death, see 'Violations of Trust,' but it is important to recall it.

Some promises I have come across in my years as a past life guide are:

"I will never leave you again."

"I will always love you."

"I will kill you!"

"I will exact my revenge in the next life." (And he did too!)

Decisions I have heard declared at the point of death are:

"I will never trust a man again."

"I will never have children."

"It's not safe to be alone."

"You can't rely on anyone."

"There will never be enough!"

"I can't trust anyone with my life – they just let you down."

"I must stay away from water."

All these statements can bring forward negative thought patterns, affect relationships and create phobias. This is why the death scene is probably the most important part of the past life experience. Many people find the idea of re-experiencing the death scene a scary prospect. Remember that you are just recalling a memory; there is nothing to be afraid of. 90% of clients I have guided through the death scene have done so without any trauma at all. Many people experience a deep sense of sadness, which passes as they leave their physical bodies. Some people are relieved when they die, as they are glad to be free of the restrictions of the world, and the encumbrance of the physical body.

Of the remaining 10%, the majority of those that have been more traumatic have been where the death has been a shock, such as by murder, or where a betrayal has occurred: death caused by a close friend or partner. However, this trauma is relatively brief. I have had comparatively few cases of very traumatic death experience, where the client has needed to physically re-experience their death to receive vital healing. In these instances I have helped the client move through the trauma to reach the understanding and lessons they needed to learn. Most people grieve as they process the death experience, staying with their body for a little while before moving off into Spirit. Here they process the information from that past life and release the unrealistic and limiting ties and promises they made.

Forgiveness is an important part of the healing process. This can be done either at the point of death, if appropriate, or just after the soul has left the body and entered Spirit. As the information about that lifetime is processed, all regrets, mistakes and any other negative associations can be understood and put into perspective. Try to forgive all those people in that past life for any harm they did you and your family or friends. At this stage of the regression you will understand that they too, were acting on their own karmic path. They too will have to go through this process when it is their time. To forgive is not always an easy thing to do, and in some cases the forgiveness comes much later, once you have had time to fully integrate the experience and effects of that past life memory. In rare cases, clients find they cannot, or will not, forgive some people, and that is a personal choice. In this instance it may take another session or two to discover what else needs to be done to enable full healing to take place for all concerned.

Likewise forgiving yourself for anything that you have done to others, or failed to do for others (see 'Widower's Guilt'), is important. You will come to understand that you cannot control everything and you cannot hold yourself responsible for things you had no control over. Sometimes you discover something awful about yourself in a past life: perhaps you murdered someone through greed or jealousy; persecuted people for their race or beliefs or discovered, like Uma's 'Viking Hatred', that you did terrible things to many other people. All your past life experiences, good and bad, are part of a larger process of learning and understanding, and you have to learn to forgive yourself. As you do your life review in Spirit, sending a message of unconditional love and saying 'sorry' to all those you may have caused harm to, intentionally or not, is a very powerful way of clearing negative feelings and karma which resonates through the past and future, for all those involved.

BETWEEN LIVES – ENTERING SPIRIT

This is another area that needs to be looked at. Most people do enter an afterlife state, once they have died in that lifetime and have 'come out' of the physical body in the past life experience, but some do not. Don't be alarmed if you do not – sometimes, particularly if the death was unexpected or traumatic, the soul will linger near the body until understanding has been reached.

I have had a glorious experience of entering the spirit world, (as have others, an example of which I have included in this book) and many experiences where I have not. I think it depends on what you need to learn from that lifetime.

It is in Spirit that you can take the time to review that past life: what you learnt from it, what you need to bring forward to the current lifetime, assess any regrets and things that you would like to change. If you want to, now is the time to rerun that lifetime and make any changes that you like, to help you move forward. This is not essential, just a matter of personal preference.

When you arrive in Spirit, you may be met by your guide, your primary soul mate or members of your soul group. More experienced souls often choose to travel alone. Most people experience a life review with their guides, here you can learn more about all your previous incarnations to date – the accumulated learning you have achieved, all the lessons you have learnt, or failed to learn. It is here also, that you will choose your next incarnation, your next family (often with those you have been with before), and you will choose what lessons and experiences you need to have in your next life. For more information about the between life state, read Michael Newton's excellent book, 'Life Between Lives' (see Further Reading).

ACCESSING YOUR PAST LIVES

Some of the techniques below take some time to get experienced enough in, to allow you to access past lives on your own. If you are just looking to experience a past life out of curiosity, then dowsing, or seeing a past life therapist, or having a psychic past life reading, may be your best option in the first instance.

I have begun with the 'traditional' or most used methods, including hypnotherapy and meditation. There are many other techniques such as bodywork, psychic card readings, dreamwork and dowsing; some more accurate and useful than others. Some methods are better for dealing with healing problems brought on by a past life, and others are fine for exploring the concept that you have lived before, without going into detail.

At the back of this book you will find information on how to find an appropriate past life guide, and a list of people and groups that offer workshops and group regressions. When undergoing a past life regression it is important to experience the lifetime, but equally important is to pass through the death scene, and into the spirit world for a deeper life review.

HYPNOTHERAPY

See 'Pregnant Nun' and 'Orkney Love Match'
Hypnosis is one of the best methods for accessing your past lives. A hypnotherapist is different from a hypnotist, in that the former can work through difficulties and help to resolve them. Hypnosis uses relaxation and guided creative visualisations to help relax the body and the conscious mind, so that the unconscious mind can access lost memories of past lives. A deep level of hypnosis is not always necessary: I can access past lives whilst in a very light state of hypnosis and for some people this light state is often all that is required.

The advantage of using hypnosis is that you will be guided into a regression, and the therapist can move you forward through the process, helping you resolve problems as they arise. The therapist can also guide you into a deeper level if required and can easily move you backwards and forwards to significant events in that lifetime. Hypnosis allows for very specific details to be recalled.

Dates, place names and other details are easily accessible, if this information is important to you. However, the therapist's questions should be open, and never be leading, nor should the therapist suggest scenarios to you.

With hypnosis the information you discover is usually automatically integrated into the conscious mind and connections with your current lifetime are made quickly. The death experience is relatively easy in hypnosis, as you can be in the event, or distanced, depending on the healing you need from that past life. Your hypnotherapist can gauge your reaction to the death experience and guide you accordingly.

A post-regression discussion is certainly useful as it helps the client to vocalise their feelings about the experience. Talking helps to process information at a deeper level and a discussion with the therapist can help clarify any difficulties in understanding. However, it is your interpretations of the experience that are important and relevant, not the therapists'. From their past experience they may be able to offer possible explanations, but they should not interpret the material for you.

Not all hypnotherapists practise past life regression and those who do practise it don't always believe in reincarnation. It is up to you to decide whether their beliefs will affect your experience. Personally, as a therapist and past life explorer, I would want to see a hypnotherapist whose beliefs mirrored my own. Personally I think that if they do not believe in reincarnation, then they cannot really understand the importance of the information I am recalling, or the significance of the healing results, and this may affect the quality of the assistance I receive.

SELF-HYPNOSIS

See 'African Healer'
This is a similar technique to hypnosis/hypnotherapy, but you do it yourself. You will need to learn self-hypnosis, which can be done in one session with a qualified hypnotherapist. This is ideal if you want to explore past life regressions frequently, and the more experienced you become at self-hypnosis, the better the experience will be. The advantage of this method is that once you have learnt the technique the sessions are free, and you can devote as much or as little time as you like to each regression. The disadvantage is that as you are alone, there will be no one to help you make the connections or help you get the past life experience into context. You also have no one to help you through any difficult or confusing images, or to guide you through the death scene. I would suggest that you don't do a past life regression alone until you are experienced in the technique of self-hypnosis, and familiar with the past life regression process.

MEDITATION

See 'The Crusader'
There are two methods of meditation: passive and active. It is important to find a method that works well for you. Meditation is a technique that can take some time to achieve successfully as it is part of a bigger ethos of spirituality. Mediation is basically about withdrawing your mind from the everyday world and finding a sacred, quiet space deep within yourself. Therein you can access your intuition and creativity, and visualise your way forward.

Passive mediation is a technique whereby you sit quietly and focus on one image, or a mantra. A mantra is a sound or the repetition of one word or short phase. The idea is that the repetition lulls you into a different state of awareness. In passive meditation you allow any images to come into your mind, and follow where they lead.

Active meditation is the focussed attention on one image or sound to the exclusion of everything else. The idea is to explore every part of that image and understand what it means literally or symbolically to you. This is not an easy state to achieve. It takes time to learn this technique, but once learnt and practised, the rewards can be significant. For the purpose of past life regression, if you have a feeling or intuition that you have had a past life in a particular time or place, then using this method and focussing on an artefact, film image or picture from this particular period can often bring surprising results.

HELPFUL MEDIATION AIDS

Many religious and spiritual cultures use a variety of aids to help reach the meditative state, and to focus the mind on achieving specific results. Singing, drumming, and dancing are used by many tribes to achieve a meditative state, often in conjunction with the local herbal hallucinogenic. (Not to be recommended for general use.)

In other societies, aroma is considered vital to help reach that altered state of consciousness to access the higher self, or past lives. Aroma is important for setting the scene as our senses transcend time: we have all had the experience when we smell a certain aroma and are suddenly transported back to childhood memories. Smell is a vital sense and there are certain incenses, or essential oils that can enhance this memory process.

INCENSE/ESSENTIAL OILS

The following incenses are listed with their appropriate assistance.

As essential oils they can be burned in an oil burner, or a drop can be placed on the temples, forehead and wrists during regression. They can also be burned as incense sticks throughout the regression session.

Lavender	relationship conflicts, reveals karmic blocks.
Frankincense	helps clarify the meaning of images.
Eucalyptus	promotes inner vision, prevents negative emotions from past life experiences.
Hyacinth	useful for birth traumas, depression.
Lilac	helps access deeper levels of consciousness & memories.
Myrrh	powerful healer, stimulates past lives that are creating blocks.
Orange	helps with emotional trauma, assists with clarity & calmness.
Sage	helps understanding and integration of information.
Sandalwood	assists accessing the focussed state.
Wisteria	stimulates memories of creativity, accesses higher vibrations.

A single oil or a combination can be used. For general use: lavender is relaxing.

CRYSTALS

Crystals can also help with the past life regression experience. They can be held in the hand, placed on the body, or tucked in the pocket during regression.

Amethyst	a meditative stone.
Carnelian	helps use past life knowledge in the present.

Hematite   helpful for hypnosis, accesses and helps with perspective.

Lapis lazuli   helps go past blocks or parts we want to resist. Helps to break harmful cycles.

MUSIC

Music can be a great help to relax you in the initial stages of regression. It is very much up to you whether you like music during a regression or not. From my experience as a therapist, I have recorded varying results: some clients found that music kept them in the present as it was a constant reminder of say, the eighteenth century forwards. Some clients found that they had a better regression experience when there was no music. Others found that very quiet music was helpful. Some kinds of music can create distraction or confusion and may break the continuity of the session, if not chosen with care.

Nature music, that is the sound of waves, birds singing etc, can be more helpful in a regression as it is timeless.

A compromise may be to have music to assist you in the relaxation process, but to ask the therapist to fade out the music as you approach the regression part of the experience. I find that this works well with clients who like some relaxing music in the initial process of the regression.

Silence is often the best accompaniment, as it offers no distractions for the unconscious mind and won't limit your creative visualisation, by having current life associations.

THE CHRISTOS METHOD

See 'Emily & Her Lost Love.'
This method requires two 'helpers', neither needs to be experienced in past life recall, but obviously it is better if you are with

someone with some knowledge or experience. This method is a combination of creative visualisation and massage-induced relaxation, much the same as hypnosis, but with physical contact. It also differs from hypnosis in that you are not aiming to enter a hypnotic state. The Christos method is more of a distraction technique, whereby the conscious mind is distracted by the massage whilst focusing on following the visualisation instructions given by one of the helpers. It is a strange and pleasant feeling, difficult to explain until you have experienced it, whereby you create a 'split' of consciousness: aware on the one hand that you are lying on the floor in the 21st century, and yet equally aware that you are experiencing a past life.

This is a very effective method, but it is complicated and time consuming, and needs two other people who are familiar with the procedure beforehand to obtain the best results.

Here is a quick 'How To' guide, for anyone who is prepared to put aside 2-3 hours to undertake it properly.

1) The 'explorer' (the person undergoing the past life regression), lies on the floor with a pillow under their head.

2) Helper one sits at the explorer's feet, and gently massages around both anklebones in a slow, circular movement. This continues for the duration of the experience, or at the very least until the explorer has regressed to a past life and this has been confirmed by appropriate questioning.

3) Helper two simultaneously massages the 'third eye' position: on the forehead just above the bridge of the nose. Pressing lightly, this area is rubbed quite briskly for several minutes, taking care not to cause discomfort. The idea is to induce a relaxed state in the explorer.

4) When the explorer is relaxed, one of the helpers can now guide the visualisation as set out below. Use a calm, softly spoken voice. The helpers should not speak unnecessarily during the relaxation and regression part of this exercise.

5) Ask the explorer to imagine he is standing in front of the door

to where he lives. Ask him to describe the door in detail. Ask the explorer to describe the front of the building where he lives.

6) Ask the explorer to imagine that he is safely and slowly rising and floating until he is standing on the roof of the building where he lives. Ask him to turn to the East, where the sun rises in the morning, and to describe what he can see from that perspective.

7) Ask the explorer, to turn to the South, and to describe everything he can see from that view. Then ask him to turn to the West and describe everything, and then ask him to turn to the North, and again, ask him to give a full description of everything he can see from this perspective. Do not rush any of these stages.

8) Then, ask the explorer whether it is day or night, and whatever the response, ask him to change the scene to the opposite. This is to re-enforce the idea that he is in control.

9) Next, ask the explorer to safely and gently continue to rise and float up into the sky, far enough so he can look down and see the whole area where he lives. Ask him to describe the scene.

10) Ask the explorer to rise safely and slowly still further up, until he is in the clouds and until he can float with the clouds and see the planet below. Ask him to describe the planet from this perspective.

11) Then ask the explorer to relax on one of the floating clouds that surround him. Tell him that he is light and weightless, that the cloud is comfortable, soft and dense, and that it can support him easily. Confirm that he is to relax and float. You can leave a gap of a few minutes now.

12) When he is secure on the cloud, inform the explorer that he is now floating back in time, through the ages, and that in a few moments, on your signal, he will be asked to leave his cloud and float down, safely and gently to Earth again. Leave a couple of minutes. Tell him that he can and will communi-

cate verbally with you at all times, and that he will respond easily to your questions.

13) Now tell the explorer that he is to rise from his cloud and as you count down from 10-0 he will float safely down to Earth and land in a past life. Reaffirm that when you reach 0 he will be in a past life. Proceed to count slowly down from 10-0.

14) When you reach 0 tell the explorer that he has now entered a past life. Tell him to feel his feet on the ground. Tell him to look at his feet and to describe what he sees.

From here, you can now ask any questions you like to fully explore this lifetime, and ask the explorer to move forward through this lifetime. If he doesn't like what he sees, remind him this is an exercise in remembering, and that he is safe. You can tell the explorer to detach himself from what he is seeing, and to imagine he is watching it on a huge TV screen. You can also tell him that he can choose to leave that past life at any time he wants, by simply opening his eyes. If the explorer says he wants to leave that past life, just tell him that he is in (the current date), and that he can wake up and leave it behind, by slowly opening his eyes when he is ready.

As this method does not take you into a hypnotic state, there is no need for an 'awakening sequence', as used in hypnosis. However, I personally like to remind the explorer of the current date and time, and allow them to control the point of alertness to the current day. As everyone is different, it is not impossible for an explorer to slip into a deeper, altered state of consciousness. This isn't a problem, just count him out by telling him to awaken gradually as you count from 1-5, and when you count 5 he will be wide awake and fully alert in (current date).

As this technique is time consuming, complicated and somewhat heavy on manpower as it were, I wouldn't recommend it for beginners. But it can be an enjoyable and beneficial experience for exploration of past lives with a group of experienced people.

OTHER METHODS

DOWSING

Dowsing is a simple, ancient technique of divining information and locating natural resources, most notably water sources and oil deposits. The same technique lends itself very well to divining past life information. It can be done alone, without any experience or prior knowledge or outside co-operation.

Almost everyone can dowse, given a relaxed yet focussed state of mind and the right equipment. Dowsing works by your unconscious mind causing involuntary muscle movements that make the pendulum move in a certain direction. Remember, you already know the information you seek, you have just forgotten it. Your unconscious mind can access it for you.

The most important aspect of dowsing for past lives is to ask clear questions that require yes or no answers.

Don't feel you have to rush out and buy expensive crystals or 'specially charged dowsing pendulums', as I recently saw being advertised in a crystal shop, for exorbitant prices. I use my favourite silver ring and a piece of white cotton thread. Some people find they can dowse with anything, others find metal objects better than crystal or glass, and for others the opposite is true. It really is a matter of personal preference. A friend of mine uses a penguin pendant on its silver chain. The best piece of advice is to take your time to discover what works best for you. If you don't get good results with one type of pendulum, try something else. A personal item or a gift with emotional significance often works best, as it is 'clued in' to your energy.

Like anything else worthwhile, dowsing is a skill that has to be learnt, and improves with practise. There is no mysticism involved with dowsing: most people can do it with a little patience.

Equipment
Try a plain silver or gold ring on a piece of cotton.
  A pendant with a fine chain.
  Your religious cross, or emblem, on string or a chain.
  A quartz crystal pendulum.
The main thing is that the pendulum whatever you choose, must hang freely, balanced from the centre, and be heavy enough to swing gently.

How to use it
Hold the string or chain in your thumb and forefinger, letting the pendulum hang down about 4-6 inches in length. Hold the pendulum over the map or resource if you are using one (see later paragraph), or over the palm of your free hand if you are doing a straightforward question and answer session.

Getting it moving
Some people believe you should 'programme' your pendulum to swing a certain way for yes and for no that you dictate. I personally believe it is easier and more appropriate to discover which way the pendulum naturally swings for yes and for no, and to go along with that. Why go against the natural inclination of your subconscious?

  Most pendulums will move in a clockwise circle for yes, and an anti-clockwise direction for no, but that isn't always the case. I have a crystal that circles clockwise for yes, and swings in a straight line for no. So, in order to determine which way the pendulum will swing for a yes response, and which way it will swing for a no response, you must ask it some questions to which you already know the answers. Asking the question aloud helps to retain clarity of thought and meaning.

  For example, to elicit a yes response I might ask one of the following questions:
  Is my name Deborah?
  Am I wearing blue jeans?

Do I live in this house?

Wait and see which way your pendulum decides to move. If the response is feeble, ask the question again, or ask for a stronger response.

Go through the same process to determine a no response. For example I may ask one of the following questions:

Am I an astronaut?

Do I live in Canada?

Do I drive a Porsche? (Good for you if you do, but I don't!)

Once you have determined which direction your pendulum swings for each response you can then ask a mixed selection of yes, no, yes, no questions, to find out how quickly your pendulum changes direction. This will happen automatically as you go through the questioning process for information about your past lives, but the speed with which the pendulum changes can vary.

You will have to pause after each question to give the pendulum time to answer. Again, if the pendulum is very slow to respond then ask for clarification, or repeat the question. You can stop the pendulum from moving at any time and then resume questioning.

If your pendulum makes a third directional movement or doesn't seem to respond clearly, there are three likely causes:

The question was ambiguous – phrase it more clearly: remember it must be a yes or no question.

Ask only one question at a time – you may already be thinking ahead to your next question and the pendulum is confused. You must keep only one question in your mind at a time.

The question may be inappropriate at the time – you may need to ask another question first.

Remember your pendulum is responding to your unconscious mind – your thoughts, and not just your voice. So it is important to concentrate on one question until you have a response.

What should I ask?

There are several ways to go about dowsing for information about past lives. By far the simplest is a straightforward question and answer technique. It may first be useful to draw up a list of questions that you want to ask. When starting to gather information about past lives, always begin with what is familiar to you. For example any strong likes or dislikes such as food, clothing styles, countries, lifestyles and civilisations etc, these could be indicators of past lives. So if you are fascinated by the Egyptian period or feel uncomfortable at the mention of the medieval era, start there. It is useful to have references handy, for example dates of historical events, lists of rulers or Pharaohs etc.

Your questions could take the form of "Did I have a past life in ancient Egypt?" Depending on the level of information you want, the resources you use would need to be detailed. In this example you might want to know under which Pharaoh's rule you lived.

If you're not bothered about specific details this may be a good way of finding out personal information. For example you could continue with questions like "Was I nobility? Was I a landowner? Was I working class? Was I female? Was I married? Was I vegetarian? Did I work on the land?" And so on.

You may like to hold your pendulum over a world map and start by asking which country you had a past life in. You could go through a history encyclopaedia's timeline, or list of significant world events. Perhaps you witnessed key events for example, wars, invasions, civilisations, natural disasters like Pompeii, or man made disasters like the Hindenburg and Titanic.

The resources you can use are inexhaustible, limited only by your time, patience and imagination. See Chapter Fourteen 'Asking Past Life Questions'.

Timeline

An easier way to get you started to discover the time periods in which you lived is to make a timeline. If you are interested in exploring the years between 1300 and 1900, take a piece of paper and write down on a horizontal line the years 1300, 1400, 1500, 1600 and so on, leaving a good inch between dates.

1300	1400	1500	1600	1700	1800	1900

Holding your pendulum over each date in turn, you can ask "Did I have a past life in this era?"

Your timeline can cover whatever dates you wish. You may then wish to do another timeline in 10 or 25-year increments, but it is simpler just to ask, "Did I live between 1500 and 1530? 1531-1560?" and break down the century in this manner.

There is no limit to the amount of personal information you can gather using this method. You can discover information about your family, your lifestyle and your friends. You can also discover how you died.

Years ago I had a job sitting in a wooden hut taking entry tickets for a car park, it was incredibly dull! Nevertheless, I took the opportunity to dowse for my past life and discovered that I had come from a well off family in Exmouth, had married the best looking man in the town and had 20 children. I also discovered that he had cheated on me with my sister, but refused to leave me for her. My sister subsequently poisoned me and within a year of my death my husband had married her.

Unfortunately for my sister he never got over my death, and she finally realised this and poisoned him. She was later caught and hung for the murder of her husband, but my murder was never discovered. I then found out that this wicked woman was actually my best friend in this life! It took the best part of the day and I had a heck of a job discovering how I died, as murder was the last thing I had thought of, but it was a fascinating process and I came up with some amazing questions in order to get answers.

If your line of questioning doesn't seem to be getting anywhere, try another angle. Or leave it, tackle a different part of that lifetime and come back to it later. Keep a notepad handy, as you will never remember all the yes/no answers.

Finding out specific information can be a long and laborious task using this method as I found out, but it is one of the best tech-

niques for a beginner to get to grips with, as you can do it alone
for free in your own time. Once you have the basic information
and if you wanted to know more specific details, you can then use
another technique to re-access that past life.

Remember one of the most important questions you need to
ask is: "Has this past life affected me negatively in my current
lifetime?"

PSYCHIC READINGS

Some psychics offer card readings to ascertain past lives that are
currently affecting you. This can be a useful starting place, giving you basic information upon which you can meditate, or use to
access at a deeper level using a number of other methods in this
chapter. Only use a psychic that is registered or on a personal recommendation. Your local Spiritualist church or their national asso-
ciation may be able to point you in the right direction. It is always
wise to avoid telephone psychics or those who claim to be able to
give an accurate reading without meeting you.

ASTROLOGY

Some astrologers can draw up past life readings from your time
and date of birth. More impressively, for those who don't know
their time of birth, some claim to be able to work backwards. That
is, given your life experiences to date they can work out your time
of birth, to within an hour. This can be a very useful method of discovering past life indicators that are influencing you now. Again,
caution should be taken to avoid exaggerated claims. Look for a
qualified astrologer, and preferably see someone who is recommended and who has a good reputation.

BODYWORK AND MASSAGE
See 'Violations of Trust'
Bearing in mind that the body stores information on a cellular level, especially regarding wounds inflicted in a past life and violent
death, often massage can arouse long forgotten memories. Spon-

taneous recall is quite common when any kind of bodywork is undertaken. Massage in itself can often trigger emotional outbursts, as the body remembers pain, distress and emotion that has been locked in the genetic memory over the centuries.

A friend of mine is a cranial osteopath and he has recorded numerous instances of clients spontaneously recalling difficult births, and pre-birth trauma, as well as hanging and decapitation deaths, when he has been working on them. Sometimes this can be distressing: particularly when non-believers experience it, or strictly religious people whose beliefs do not include reincarnation.

However, with care and sensitivity these experiences can provide valuable insights into your current life difficulties.

AUDIOTAPES AND CDS
See 'Widower's Guilt'
There are many audiocassettes and CDs on the market offering guided past life regressions from 20-40 minutes in length. The methods used to access your past lives usually include full body relaxation, some hypnosis deepening techniques and creative visualisation. The value of these guided audio methods is varied. I have personally used audio methods as a way of learning, relaxation, meditation, self-improvement and for accessing past life memories, with varying degrees of satisfaction.

I am very careful about which ones I choose. For past life work, I have used Denise Linn's excellent tapes, as listed at the end of this book. I tend to buy those tapes recorded by people whose work I have read, or whose workshops I have attended. I have purchased tapes by people I don't know, but have twice been disappointed. The first time I just didn't like the man's voice and although I persevered, I eventually gave up as his voice grated on my nerves, distracting me. The second time I found that I just didn't agree with the ethos and methodology the woman used for regression.

The disadvantages of audiocassettes are time and flexibility. There is never enough time to fully explore the past life you discover, and although Denise Linn gives you some time to go back and change anything that disturbs you, others do not. As for flexibility, you may not have fully relaxed before the tape guides you into the next stage. There is no problem with this other than you may feel 'left behind' and this in turn may affect your enjoyment and ability to concentrate. With a second person to guide you, they can judge how quickly or slowly to take the process: with audio methods this is not available.

However, they are certainly a good introduction to accessing past lives. Some authors warn you against using this method, but I would just say that if you use a therapist's tape and aim to experience a positive past life, then it is unlikely that you will have a problem. If you are still unsure, arrange to have a friend to sit with you, who can help you through anything difficult that may arise. In my experience, pre-programming the idea of having a positive life experience usually leads the subconscious to show you just that. Bear in mind that the more experience you have of opening your subconscious to meditation, hypnosis and past life exploration, the better you are able to cope with 'going solo'.

When considering using this method to explore past lives either use a product by a well known and well established professional in the field, or go by a personal recommendation.

DREAMWORK
See 'An American Dream'
This method is one of my personal favourites. Dreams are very powerful tools of the unconscious, and a lot of the everyday 'stuff' we encounter is filtered and processed at night whilst we sleep, during dreams. It is not uncommon for past lives to occur in dream format, as we can process them as we sleep. Something that has happened during the day may trigger a past life dream: often deja vu, or a particular activity or situation will also recall a past life under similar circumstances.

Past life dreams are separate and unique from regular dreams and as such they are instantly recognisable. They are usually more intense, brightly coloured and evoke powerful emotions. Recurring dreams can often be traced back to a past life cause – these dreams are trying to get a message to you.

Messages from people in Spirit are also common. A soul in Spirit can comfort the dreamer, and offer advice and warnings about difficult times ahead. Dreamtime is an important place where the boundaries between Earth, Spirit and other realms are merged. It is here that some people astral travel.

Programming Dreams

You can try to programme dreams for past life information. If you have already picked up basic information through dowsing, psychic cards or from having had a regression, you can use dream programming to further explore that life in detail.

Just before you go to bed, place an amethyst crystal under your pillow.

Lie comfortably and take a few deep breaths to help you relax.

Replay the information you have in your mind, in story form or as if you are watching a film. Where there are gaps, invent the information. As Denise Linn says in her book 'Past Lives, Present Dreams': "Imagination is the pump that primes the past." (See Further Reading.) So use your imagination, and the rest will follow. You may have to run through this process a couple of times and then allow yourself to drift off to sleep with the intention to discover more, and recall upon awakening.

If you have no previous information and want to try and recall a past life through dreams try the following technique.

1) Just before you go to bed, place an amethyst crystal under your pillow.

2) Lie comfortably and take a few deep breaths to help you relax.

3) Using a place or time period that you are attracted to, or know a lot about, create a scenario, allow your imagination to start you off. Follow the thread of whatever appears, and if you encounter gaps – invent the next bit.

4) Allow yourself to drift off to sleep. What will most likely

happen is that your unconscious mind will take over the images and direct you to a relevant past life.

If the images start to change unaided before you drift into sleep, then go with them: this is your unconscious mind taking over.

Keep a notepad and pencil by your bed and record any images or emotions as soon as you wake up. Jotting down a few keywords as soon as you can will allow you to go back to sleep, and recall the dream in full when you wake up properly. If you wait until you are fully awake you may forget the information!

GROUP WORKSHOPS
See 'Victorian Connections' and 'The Alcoholic'
These are a great way to sample a past life relatively cheaply, with the support of a group environment and led by a professional. There are several groups around the country that run seminars and workshops and you will find details of a few of them at the end of this book. Groups usually use a combination of creative visualisation and guided relaxation. Some group leaders use extras like art and drama.

The only drawback is that group sessions or workshops seldom allow the opportunity for one on one discussion with the therapist, and rarely allow for in-depth healing of any problems that you may discover are affecting you in the current lifetime. It is unusual for anything very traumatic to arise during a group regression, but if it does the therapist and assistants should be qualified and capable of dealing with it. It is worth asking about this before you book. This method is another good way of getting basic information that you can explore further in your own time, with or without the help of a professional.

Whichever method you choose, take your time to explore all those that you feel comfortable with. Each method has its own advantages and drawbacks.

CHAPTER FOURTEEN

INTERACTIVE: ASKING PAST LIFE QUESTIONS & PAST LIFE INDICATOR QUESTIONNAIRE

There are many questions you can ask limited only by your time and imagination. Generally speaking it is better to use basic questioning skills to get started, and then let the explorer's answers guide the direction of your remaining questions.

Sometimes the explorer may be reticent or brusque in their response, in which case you can ask for more detailed replies. This doesn't always work. When I was training, my colleague Steve regressed to a hard lifetime as a Yorkshire miner. He was a grumpy old so and so! No matter what I asked he gave monosyllabic answers and responded like I was an idiot asking ridiculous questions. Whilst the experience was highly amusing, I felt intrusive and uncomfortable. In some circumstances you are best served to focus on the healing aspects of the regression.

Firstly start by focussing on the feet as this helps to ground the experience. Ask the explorer to look at his feet. The questions you ask may run as follows, but remember to go by the responses you receive, and feel free to further question any leads they give you. It is a bit like an investigation!

Good phrases to use are "Where are you now?" "Tell me what you see." "Describe what you see." "Move forward to the next significant event in that life." "How do you feel about that?"

SAMPLE QUESTIONS –
FILL IN BELOW OR COPY YOUR ANSWERS
ONTO A SEPARATE SHEET

Concentrate on your feet. Describe your feet.

Are you wearing anything on your feet or are they bare?

If yes:
What colour are they?

What are they made of?

How do they feel?

What are you standing on?

Describe it.

Become aware of where you are.
Are you indoors or outdoors?

Look at your clothing.
What are you wearing?

How does it feel?

Is it rough or smooth?

Are you warm or cold?

What is the weather like?

Are you carrying or holding anything?
(If yes)
What is it?

What is in it?

What are these things for?

Look at your hands.
Describe them.

Are you wearing any jewellery?
Describe it.

Put your hands up to feel your head.
Do you have hair?

Describe it.

Do you have anything on your head?
Describe it.

Now focus on what is going on around you.
Are you alone or are there other people here?
Tell me what you see.

Do you recognise anyone?

Can you hear anything?

Can you smell anything?

Can you hear voices?

What are they saying?

Become aware of the sounds and smells around you.
Describe them.

Is this place fertile or barren land?

Is it flat, hilly, mountainous or something else?

Describe everything you can see.

Where are you?

What is the name of this place?

Are there trees and flowers around you?
Describe them:

What is the year?

What is the season?

Who rules you?

What are you doing here?

What is your name?

Do you have a family?

Where is your family?

How do you feel in this body?

Are you healthy or sick?

Is there anything wrong with you or are you fit?

How old are you?

Move forward to a time where you are standing outside the place
that you live.
Describe what you see.

How do you feel about your home?

Do you live alone or with others?

Who are they?

What is your connection to these people?

Explore your home, describe what you see:

If you are already indoors then:
Go to a window or door and tell me what you can see outside.

Go to a time when you are eating your evening meal.
What are you eating?

Where are you?

Go to a time when you go to get supplies:
How do you get there?

Where are you?

Describe what you see.

How do you pay for your goods?

If money – look at where you keep your money, describe it.

What do you pay with?
Describe your currency.

If you don't have money, how do you trade?

What do you buy here?

To move the explorer forward in the lifetime:
Go to the next significant event.

Where are you?

To go to the death scene:
Go to the day before you die.

Where are you?

How do you feel?

Is there anything going on around you?

Go to the hour before you die.
Where are you?

How do you feel?

Are you alone or are others with you?

Who are they?

Do you recognise them in your current life?

What is happening to you?

Is there any other event in that lifetime that you need to go back and review?
(If so tell them to quickly do it)

If not:
How do you feel about dying?

Is there anything else that concerns you?

What have you learnt in this lifetime?

Do you have any regrets?

What are you thinking?

What would you change?

Go through the death experience. Allow that body to die and see yourself leaving that body and rising above it.
How do you feel now?

How do you feel about leaving that body?

What have you learnt from that lifetime that can help you in your current life?

What advice would you give yourself to help you now?

If there is anything that you want to change in that lifetime? You have a short time to do that now.

The information you get from the hour before dying to the end of the session is often the most important from the healing point of view. It is important to make sure that any issues are resolved and let go of. The opportunity for the explorer to go back and change anything they like helps to process the past life, heal the trauma, and let go of any limiting beliefs that may have been carried forward.

PAST LIFE INDICATORS QUESTIONNAIRE

At the beginning of this book I mentioned that strong likes and dislikes were good indicators of past life information. Below is a questionnaire that will help focus your mind on specific information, which may give you clues to your own past lives. This is loosely based on Denise Linn's similar exercise for past life exploration.

Fill in your answers below or make your own notes on a piece of paper to the following headings:

Childhood games

Childhood habits

Clothing styles

Architecture

Favourite foods

Food dislikes

Food allergies

Pain you have experienced (especially recurring)

Operations

Illnesses

Fears/Phobias

Scars/birthmarks

Geographical likes

Geographical dislikes

Climates you like

Climates you dislike

Cultures that appeal to you

Cultures that repel you

Time periods/historical events that appeal to you

Time periods/historical events that repel you

Deja vu experiences

Occupations you have had

Aspirations you have

Talents/abilities

Race/Heritage and family connections

Special people you feel strongly for

People you feel strongly against or dislike

Books and movies

Animals and pets

Personality and mannerisms

Repetitive dreams

The responses to these headings may give you strong indicators of past life interests, skills and lifestyles. It certainly gives you a good place to start.

CONCLUSION

As I said at the beginning, this book is intended to demonstrate the immense value and understanding that comes from keeping an open mind about reincarnation and past lives. So much healing has been received from so many people not only in England but all around the world, which leads me to believe that past life therapy is the key to understanding our inner motives and our spiritual selves.

Dying has always fascinated me, and deep down I suspected it wasn't the end, but the middle: one part of a journey. Now I am certain of it.

I hope that this book has given you food for thought, and a desire to seek answers for yourself. Hopefully it will inspire you to make your own journey of discovery.

When looking at your past lives it is important to remember that they all reflect each other and affect each other: in accumulation they have made you who you are today, the bits you are proud of, and your shadow side too. You have the power and inner knowledge to change those parts of you that you are not so proud of, if you want to. Your shadow side has as much to teach you, as your light side.

Blessings to you all.

Deborah

FINDING A THERAPIST

CONTACTS

FURTHER READING

ABOUT THE AUTHOR

ACKNOWLEDGEMENTS

FINDING A THERAPIST

There are trained Past Life Therapists, but they are not always easy to find. Some hypnotherapists offer Past Life Regression Therapy (PLRT), but don't openly advertise it: some believe it would negatively reflect on the perceived professionalism of their business. Some past life therapists can help you access a past life, but are not trained to deal with the death scene, between lives, or processing the trauma that is affecting the current life. You do not really want not be in a situation where you have unearthed an issue that needs resolving, only to find that the therapist is incapable of dealing with it.

You may like to start with the telephone book and just talk to people. Finding out what they are qualified to do and how much experience they have is very important. It is easier to discover if you 'connect' with that person or not. Generally go with your gut feeling: if someone doesn't seem to be on your wavelength then they won't be a good therapist for you.

Try not to judge a therapist solely on price. Some of the more expensive therapists have a more in-depth regression programme, whilst others are just greedy. PLRT is a specialist area often combining knowledge of hypnosis, counselling and psychoanalysis, as well as advanced spiritual understanding, so the cheaper therapists may just not be qualified, experienced or capable of dealing with traumatic events, should they arise. At current prices (2006) a 2-hour session costing between £70-80 is fair.

Find out what a session consists of, how it is structured, whether the therapist will guide you through the death experience and into Spirit, and the proportion of time spent in each. Ask if they will stop at one past life or enter another if there is time remaining? Ask what they believe in, and whether they are trained for past life therapy as well as regression. Can they help you process any problems that may arise?

Allow at least 2 hours, anything less isn't going to be a comprehensive session. Ask what methods they use to access the past life and the kind of questions they ask. Do they offer a taped recording of your session? Although it is not necessary, as you will remember everything, it is a nice bonus.

CONTACTS

USEFUL CONTACTS FOR FINDING A THERAPIST

Corsebar Hypnotherapy Training School
Corsebar Road
Paisley
Scotland
PA2 9PY
0141 8421470
www.learn-hypnosis.co.uk
corsebar@yahoo.co.uk

Directory of Past Life Therapists
PO BOX 26
London
WC2H 9LP

The online Holistic Dictionary
www.holisticdirectory.co.uk

Vicki & Neil Watson
Founder of National Society of Professional Hypnotherapists
www.learn-hypnosis.co.uk

PUBLIC WORKSHOPS & SEMINARS

Deborah J Monshin
Grumbleknot
Yealm Park
Yealmpton
Devon
PL8 2NS
01752 880880
www.devonhypnosis.co.uk
pastliferesearch@yahoo.co.uk

Denise Linn Seminars
PO Box 759
Paso Robles,
California
USA
93447
www.deniselinn.com
sacredoak33@aol.com

Roger Woolger
Briarwood
Long Wittenham
Oxford
OX14 4QW
www.rogerwoolger.com

Dr Michael Newton PhD
C/O Llewellyn Publishing Worldwide
PO Box 64383
Dept. 0738704652
St Paul
MN
55164-0383
USA
www.llewellyn.com

THERAPIST TRAINING ESTABLISHMENTS

Corsebar Hypnotherapy Training School
Corsebar Road
Paisley
Scotland
PA2 9PY
0141 8421470
www.learn-hypnosis.co.uk
corsebar@yahoo.co.uk

Dominic Beirne School of Clinical Hypnosis and Psychotherapy
The Stables
Welcombe Road
Stratford upon Avon
Warwickshire
CV37 6UJ
01789 261620
www.hypnosis-nlp.co.uk
info@hypnosis-nlp.co.uk

Lionheart Training
Steve Burgess at Natural Therapy Ltd
Beverley Natural Therapy Centre
17, Barleyholme Wharf,
Beverley
Hull
17 0FD
www.steveburgesshypnosis.com
steve@naturaltherapy.karoo.co.uk

Roger Woolger
Briarwood
Long Wittenham
Oxford OX14 4QW
01865 407996
www.rogerwoolger.com

Institute of Clinical Hypnosis
28 Tantallon Road
London
SW12 8DG
www.ichypnosis.co.uk

FURTHER READING

Denise Linn
'Past Lives, Present Dreams' Piatkus, ISBN 0749913770
Audiocassettes: 'Past Lives and Beyond.' QED 118. ISBN 01914118005

Judy Hall
'Past Life Therapy', Thorsons, ISBN 0722533535
'Deja Who?' Findhorn, ISBN 1899171525

Dr. Brian Weiss
'Many Lives, Many Masters' Piatkus, ISBN 0749913789
'Through Time into Healing' Piatkus, ISBN 0749918357

Roger J Woolger
'Other Lives, Other Selves.' Thorsons, ISBN 185538311x

Carol Bowman
'Children's Past Lives.' Element, ISBN 186204354x

Raymond Moody
'Life after Life.' Bantam, ISBN 0712602739

Ian Stevenson
'Twenty Cases Suggestive of Reincarnation.' University Press, ISBN 0813908728

Jenny Cockell
'Yesterday's Children.' Piatkus, ISBN 0749912464

Michael Newton PhD
'Journey of Souls.' Llewellyn, ISBN 1567184855
'Destiny of Souls.' Llewellyn, ISBN 1567184995
'Life Between Lives.' Llewellyn, ISBN 0739704652

Brandon Bays
'The Journey.' Thorsons, ISBN 000717490x

ACKNOWLEDGEMENTS

I would like to express my heartfelt thanks and deep appreciation for all those generous people who have contributed their wonderful experiences for us all to share. I hope that they have benefited from reliving their past life memories, as much as you have been inspired by their journeys.

It has been a great privilege for me to work with these wonderful people to bring this book to fulfilment.

As past life memories are very personal insights, I hope that you respect the privacy of those that chose not to be named. I am just grateful that they agreed to share their memories with us.

My thanks and blessings to the contributors:

Clare Hawtin, Catherine Lucas, Amanda Poyner, Lynda Shaw, Uma, and those who wished to remain anonymous.

My heartfelt thanks to Denise Linn and Dominic Beirne for generously endorsing my book, and to Vicki Watson for her wonderful foreword.

Also thank you to:

Christina Hanley, Natalie Hanley, Matthew Dowson, Lynda Shaw, Audrey Monshin & John Monshin for their help and support in making this book happen. And to Jeremy Nelson and James Cook at Trafford Publishing for all their expert advice.

Cover jacket design & text by Deborah J Monshin.

I am planning another book, as so much more needs to be explored and explained.

If you are interested in contributing your stories, please contact me at:

 hlemag@gmail.com

ISBN 141208385-0